1992

P9-CDX-733

Extraordinary Hispanic Americans

Extraordinary Hispanic Americans

By Susan Sinnott

Consultants

George Blanksten, Ph.D.
Professor Emeritus, Department of Political Science
Northwestern University
Evanston, Illinois

Teresa Longo, Ph.D.
Assistant Professor, Department of Modern Languages and Literatures
College of William and Mary
Williamsburg, Virginia

Arthur Olivas
Museum of New Mexico
Santa Fe, New Mexico

CHILDRENS PRESS®
CHICAGO

Dedication

To my son Nathaniel Wackman who just turned seven and is a "wicked good" reader, and to Charnan Simon, another great reader and writer and friend.

Project editor: E. Russell Primm III
Editorial assistance: Alice Rubio
Designer: Lindaanne Donohoe
Photo research: Judith Feldman
Indexer: Kathryn Cairns
Proofreaders: Irene B. Keller, Sara Guth
Cover mural: Oscar Romero

Picture acknowledgments appear on pages 273 and 274

Library of Congress Cataloging-in-Publication Data

Sinnott, Susan.
   Extraordinary Hispanic Americans / by Susan Sinnott.
     p. cm.
   Summary: Profiles the lives of Hispanics who helped shape
the history of the United States.
   ISBN 0-516-00582-0
   1. Hispanic Americans—History—Juvenile literature. 2.
United States—Civilization—Spanish influences—Juvenile
literature. [1. Hispanic Americans—Biography. 2. United
States—Civilization—Spanish influences.] I. Title.
E184.S75S55 1991   91-13909
973'.0468—dc20   CIP
                                AC

Table of Contents

Foreword

The problem starts with the word "Hispanic," which according to the dictionary refers to the language, people, and culture of Spain. Far from helping to identify this diverse ethnic group, the term itself seems to cloud our understanding. What about the Africans of Cuba and Puerto Rico and the Indians of Central America? Can they all be lumped together as "Hispanics"? Add "Americans" to the title and clarity becomes a dot on the horizon. What's an American, after all, if not a hodgepodge of the world's races and nationalities and religions? What then is the reader to make of a book whose three-word title features two words that defy precise definition? *Extraordinary Hispanic Americans* may seem to some, I'm afraid, a maddening blend of unconnected people and events. Other readers, I hope, will enjoy the book for what is, for lack of a better word, its "muralistic" view of history.

Murals are to twentieth century Mexican art what sculpture was to Renaissance Italy. The great Mexican muralists of the 1920s and 1930s, such as Diego Rivera and José Clemente Orozco, grabbed the world's attention with their boisterous, gutsy paintings that depicted life and death in New World. These artists were, in effect, giving notice to the European art world that from now on Mexico would play by its own rules. Here, they said, we don't worry so much about order and tidiness; here we don't hide our rough edges.

Art observers discovered that the mural was indeed the perfect form for "reading" the history of the New World. Murals are very hospitable, welcoming both the unexpected and incongruous. Heroes can stand shoulder to shoulder with ordinary people. A scoundrel or two—or many—can be added for good measure. The story can be read from left to right or right to left, or, one can jump into the middle and head off in either direction.

So, too, when reading a book that tries to take in the history of the Spanish-speaking peoples of the United States, there are no ground rules except to start with a wide-open mind. Read a few of the biographies carefully, then stand back and place them within the larger picture. Appreciate a category as unwieldy as "Hispanic Americans" for its sheer vastness.

My hope is that the biographies will be like splashes of color that, when taken together, will become, if not a great painting, at least something meaningful and enlightening. The history of Hispanic America is, of course, fascinating and overwhelming and elusive. The challenge for both the teller and the reader is to grasp the essence of a moving, changing, vigorous people, who seem to defy the limitations of canvas or paper.

Susan Sinnott
Portsmouth, New Hampshire
June 1991

Note to the Reader

Whenever the birth and death dates for a person are known they have been included. Sometimes the dates are less than certain or are completely unknown. Those dates followed with a question mark indicate a lack of certainty about the probable date cited. A lesser degree of certainty is indicated by the abbreviation *c.* (for the Latin *circa* meaning about or approximately) before the date. A question mark with no date attached at all indicates absolute uncertainty.

In most instances, the spelling of proper names follows Spanish grammar (including the accent markings). Names of people and places that have become anglicized, however, are spelled without accent markings. For example, Jacob Rodríquez Rivera's name is spelled with a grave accent while Richard Rodriquez's name is not accented.

Part One

An Age of Exploration

S pain's great explorers of the late 1400s and the 1500s were really just team players in a very serious game. The Spanish were one of four—there were also the Portuguese, French, and English—and they all played by the same rules, that is, by no rules at all. Whoever could discover and claim the most land, using whatever means necessary, would make their own country the most powerful on earth.

The Portuguese got off to an early lead. In the 1440s, Prince Henry the Navigator became the first to attempt finding a sea route to the Indies. He headed off in the two most likely directions. First, he went east and around the coast of Africa. Next, he headed west across the Atlantic Ocean. He reached the Azores, 900 miles west of Portugal, but went no farther.

At the time of Prince Henry's death in 1460, Portugal had the most skilled mapmakers, geographers, and navigators in Europe. Consequently, when a young man from Genoa, Italy, named Christopher Columbus wanted to realize his own dream of finding a sea route to India, he went first to Portugal, both to learn from their skilled seamen and to seek financial support for his own mission.

Columbus begged Portugal's royal family for their support but was turned down. Finally, Columbus went to Spain where Queen Isabella I listened sympathetically to his plan. In the end, though she, too, turned him down. She was eager to show the world what great mariners the Spanish were. But why should she entrust such an undertaking to an Italian?

Columbus remained in Spain for six years after his first meeting with Isabella. In 1492, he again appeared at court to ask for royal sponsorship. He stated his terms and, in effect, told the king and queen, take it or leave it. Leave it they did, and Columbus decided to leave, too, for France. A day later, however, the queen changed her mind. The queen's messenger hurried to find the sailor and bring him back. He found Columbus on a dusty road a few miles north, traveling by mule to the French capital. Much to Christopher Columbus's amazement, the king and queen of Spain had agreed to fully fund his attempt to become the "Admiral of the Ocean Sea."

When Columbus set sail in August 1492, he commanded three Spanish ships and a crew of ninety. This Italian mariner was about to encounter what would one day be called North America. As the fifteenth century became the sixteenth, there would be one clear leader in high-stakes quest for world power—Spain.

Christopher Columbus and his crew landing in the New World.

Columbus's Crew

When, in 1492, Christopher Columbus finally received the support of the Spanish crown for his daring voyage, he traveled to the port of Palos to outfit his fleet and recruit men. Palos—on the southwest coast of Spain, very near Portugal—was the home of two famous shipping families, the Pinzóns and the Niños, and they were eager to help Columbus. From the Niño family, came the Niña, Columbus's favorite ship. The Pinzón brothers, Martin Alonso and Vicente Yáñez, became captains of the *Pinta* and the *Niña*, respectively. Columbus himself took control of the *Santa María*, a fine ship from the province of Galicia in northern Spain.

Recruiting sailors proved, at first, much more difficult than finding ships. Local seamen gathered in Palos's town square and talked among themselves about whether to sign on. Many could not see why they should risk their lives on the slight chance they might be able to find a sea route to the Indies. There might be rich new lands in between, but there might also be nothing, just the end of the earth. The Portuguese, they knew, had sailed west to India and found nothing. If the skilled Portuguese captains had failed, why did this Italian think he would be the one to succeed?

Then one day a grizzled old sailor came to the main square of Palos and started talking to the reluctant recruits. "Seize this chance," he told them, "you may never have another." The old man's name was Pedro Vásques de la Frontera, and forty years before he had sailed on one of the Portuguese voyages of discovery. Although his ship had also turned back from the western seas, he was absolutely certain he'd been near the mythical island of Brazil. "Before the fog fell," he said, "I saw rocks of gold. Go, you will all become rich men! The land is there—why, if I were twenty years younger, I'd go too!" Nearly ninety men followed the ancient mariner's advice and signed on. All but four members of the three ships' crews were Spaniards. These men were the first of the many, many thousands from all over Spain and the rest of Europe, who, after hearing the stories of Columbus's sailors, would decide to leave their lives of poverty at home and instead search for gold and riches and adventure!

Martin Alonzo Pinzón searches for land from the rigging of the Pinta

The Conquistadors

News of Columbus's arrival in the New World in 1492 was of special interest to the soldiers of Spain. They were a well-trained, well-armed group, notorious for their brutality. Since early that same year, when Spain had defeated the Moors at Granada and ended centuries of war, they'd had little to do. When word arrived from Columbus's expeditions of whole new continents, many of these conquistadors wasted no time raising armies and heading west into the unknown.

They were a reckless group of invaders who seemed to have nothing to fear from the unknown jungles, mountains, and prairies they marched into. They fought constantly against both the elements (a brutal and unfamiliar climate) and hostile Indian tribes. They overran the Indian populations with dizzying speed, and in fifty years they had taken much of South and Central America (areas that are now called Cuba, Panama, Venezuela, Mexico, Peru, Ecuador, Paraguay, and Chile).

What drove them? Many just longed for adventure and were unfazed by the risks and dangers. Some honestly hoped to convert the natives to Christianity. Still others faced persecution at home and saw the conquest of new lands as one way to escape. All hoped to find the wealth and power they knew they could never have in Spain.

Many conquistadors were also chasing dreams, literally. There was so much that was new and different: jungles filled with colorful birds that the natives could teach to talk, crickets that chirped through the night, and tall, handsome people who were covered with gold jewelry. Because they could see such wonders up close, they believed such fantastic places as the Fountain of Youth or El Dorado or the Seven Cities of Cíbola couldn't be far away either.

As the conquistadors poured into the Americas in the years following Columbus's voyages, the successes of a few became well known. There were Cortés and Pizarro, to name two, who had overtaken Mexico and Peru, respectively, and had returned home wealthy, powerful men.

These early successes, however, were not easy to copy. The swift and total victory that the Spaniards enjoyed in Central America did not come as easily once the soldiers moved into North America. In Mexico and Peru, the native people (named "Indians" by the Europeans who believed they arrived in India) had fought well but had been overrun as the Spanish soldiers with their armor and steel weapons and horses pressed on ruthlessly.

In North America, however, the native people were not as easily overcome. The Spaniards' heavy steel weapons quickly became embarrassingly awkward. As soldiers stopped to take aim, the skilled Indian archers would dash from tree to tree. Arrows flew around the Spaniards. As these hit-and-run attacks became more frequent, panic set in. Instead of moving ever forward as the conquistadors had in Central America, they began to scatter and retreat. Under such conditions the resolve of even the most courageous conquistadors was greatly tested.

Juan Ponce de León

Explorer

1460–1521

Juan Ponce de León was a restless, young Spanish nobleman who, in 1493, volunteered to accompany Columbus on his Second Voyage. The fleet dropped anchor on the western coast of Puerto Rico, and Ponce de León, drawn to the rich soil of the Añasco Valley and the lovely limestone hills, decided to settle. He no doubt was also interested in rumors that the island was rich in gold.

In 1509, the Spanish Crown named Ponce de León governor of Puerto Rico. Within three years, he was very rich and in complete control of the island. He was not an especially kind ruler, however. One observer of the time wrote that Ponce de León grew rich on "the labors, blood and sufferings of his subjects," meaning that after conquering the island's natives, he stole their gold for himself.

Ponce was finally replaced as governor in 1513 by Christopher Columbus's son, D. Diego Colón. The king of Spain, to pacify Ponce who felt he'd been treated badly by Columbus, gave the deposed governor a grant to discover new lands in the New World.

Ponce was delighted with the king's gift. He'd heard much of the Fountain of Youth, whose waters were said to make old men young again, from local Indians. The Fountain, they said, is on the Great Island to the north. Ponce was eager to begin his search for the magical waters.

In early March 1513, Ponce de León left Puerto Rico with three small ships. Ponce and his crew passed Eleuthera in the Bahamas on Easter Sunday, March 27. On April 2, they spotted the shores of the Great Island and sought shelter from a fierce storm in one of its harbors. The strange new land was flat and full of groves; its sweet-smelling flowers nearly intoxicated the sailors. Ponce thought it appropriate to name the lovely place "Florida," both to honor its flowery scent and after the Spanish name for Holy Week, *Pascua Florida*.

The fleet had landed near what is today called Daytona Beach. Ponce and his ships then headed south along the coast. Whenever they saw natives on shore, the Spaniards stopped and asked where they could find the Fountain of Youth. They passed what we know today as Cape Canaveral, Palm Beach, Fort Lauderdale, Miami, and the Florida Keys. All along the way, the men gathered the water in casks and drank as much as they could. But there were no miracles, no Fountain of Youth.

By June 1513, Ponce de León had given up on the Fountain and took on an Indian guide to direct the fleet back to Puerto Rico. The young native man sent them off course, and, instead of passing south of Cuba as Ponce wanted, the ships landed off the Yucatán Peninsula of Mexico. When the captain and his men walked on shore, they became the first Spaniards to set foot in Central America.

Ponce returned to Florida about eight years later. Even though he was past sixty, he was no longer interested in the Fountain of Youth. Now he wanted to start a colony. This would be, he felt, his last chance to become very wealthy and powerful. He landed near present-day Fort Myers and immediately began trading goods with the Indians.

Ponce de León's troubles with the natives of the New World are legendary. In a word, he was brutal. Why was it that other Spaniards who came to Florida later found the Indians friendly and even helpful? Unfortunately, Ponce never learned that his colony could not succeed without the support of the native people. He battled with them constantly, until, finally, he himself was struck by an arrow. His men took their wounded leader to Cuba for medical help, and Ponce de León died in Havana in July 1521.

Ponce de León and his men search for the elusive Fountain of Youth.

Antón de Alaminos

Pilot to the Conquistadors

(lifedates unknown)

If the history of the exploration of the New World were written not about the men who commanded ships and led soldiers but about those who piloted the ships, Antón de Alaminos would be as famous as Christopher Columbus.

Antón de Alaminos was a native of Palos, the Spanish port that provided Columbus with his ships and crew. Alaminos first sailed to the New World as a boy on Columbus's Second Voyage (1493–96), then later as a pilot on the Last Voyage (1502–04) when the mainland of Central America was charted for the first time. By 1512, when Antón became the pilot of one of Ponce de León's ships, he knew the coasts, currents, and winds of the Caribbean and Gulf of Mexico extremely well.

He understood them so well, in fact, that he became the first to point out the existence of a phenomenon that we call the Gulf Stream. The Gulf Stream is the narrow high-speed ocean current that travels first north from the Caribbean Sea then along the Florida and Carolina coast, before veering east at Cape Hatteras, North Carolina. It separates the cool coastal waters from the warmer Sargasso Sea in the mid-Atlantic. Once the path of the Gulf Stream was discovered, ships could use it to give them a boost as they traveled north and east from the Caribbean. Ships traveling from European ports west would avoid the Gulf Stream, as its counter-current slowed them down.

When Antón piloted Ponce de León's ship from Puerto Rico to the north, he headed in a northwesterly direction so that he could ride the Gulf Stream. When his ship sailed south from its first landing at present-day Daytona Beach, he skillfully hugged the coast so that he could take advantage of the southward coastal drift. Once the expedition reached the sandy stretch now called Cape Canaveral, where seas and winds clash, the countercurrent of the powerful Gulf Stream slowed the ships considerably. Because of the strong currents, it took twice as long for Ponce de León's ships in 1513 to travel from St. Augustine, Florida, to the Florida Keys as it did for the entire trip from Puerto Rico to St. Augustine.

Later, as Alaminos piloted ships into the Gulf of Mexico and along the Central American coast, he was able to apply his knowledge of the winds and currents to steer the best possible course between the Indies and Spain. He served not only Columbus and Ponce de León but later, in 1518, he piloted Juan de Grijalba from Cuba to the Yucatán in Mexico. Then, in 1519, he guided Cortés to the riches of Mexico. Antón de Alaminos died in Spain in 1520.

Columbus's ships: The Santa Maria, Niña, *and* Pinta

Lucas Vázquez de Ayllón
Sugar-Mill Owner, Explorer
*c.*1475–1526

The Spanish had every reason to believe the sugar mills that they established on the island of Hispaniola would make them rich. Sugar cane grew well in the Caribbean, and there was a great demand for the product in Spain. What stood in the way, the Spanish monarch wondered, of producing as much as the people of Europe could want?

The problem was labor. There was no one, it seemed, to work the mills. Black slaves were expensive, and the natives of the island had all but died out. To make matters worse, ruthless slave hunters had wiped out Indian populations on other islands, too. Clearly, the mill owners would need to look elsewhere for the workers they so badly needed.

Two ships left Hispaniola in 1521, sailed north to the mainland, and up the coast to an area the Spanish called Chicora (today the site of Charleston, South Carolina). There were many Indians in Chicora, and they were very curious when the Spanish ships arrived. The Spaniards had brought presents from their king, and they invited the Indians aboard ship to receive them. Just as the ships were filled with guests, however, the sails went up and the Spaniards headed for Hispaniola. For a while anyway, the sugar mills would have the workers they needed.

One of the sugar-mill owners was a man named Lucas Vázquez de Ayllón. As the captured Indians were divided up, Ayllón took one who seemed particularly bright to be his personal assistant. He renamed the man Francisco Chicora. Francisco learned Spanish quickly and traveled to Spain with Ayllón, where he told the court at Seville about the wonderland of Chicora. The land is very fertile, he told his audience; it's filled with trees and plants just like those of Spain. There are many tribes of very smart people, he went on, ruled by one gigantic man. What's more, you can find pearls the size of fists almost everywhere.

It sounded too good to be true, and, unfortunately for Ayllón, it was. Francisco desperately wanted to go back home and hoped his stories would speed up his return. The Spanish, he thought, would want to settle in this wondrous place as quickly as possible. Just as Francisco hoped, Ayllón completely believed the stories and asked the Spanish crown to let him try to establish a colony in Chicora.

Ayllón didn't realize his mistake until July 1526 when he, six ships, five hundred men, and ninety horses landed on the Georgia coast. Chicora didn't look at all like Spain: Spain is dry and fertile; Chicora was low and flat and swampy. The humidity was nearly unbearable.

To make matters worse, Ayllón's flagship, which he had foolishly loaded with nearly all the expedition's food and supplies, ran aground as it entered the Río Jordán (today the Santee River). Both the ship and supplies were lost; the colony of Chicora was in poverty from the start. Shortly afterwards, Francisco and the other Indians on board ran away and were never seen again. Now the Spaniards not only were without food, but they also had no guides or interpreters.

The Spaniards abandoned their sailing ships and set off down the coast in much smaller vessels. They eventually reached a large river that they called the Guadalupe—it is now the Savannah. They decided to set up camp at the head of the river, at the site of Savannah, Georgia.

The new colony didn't have to worry about food, despite the loss of their provisions. The area's vegetation and animal life were rich and varied. There were chestnut and walnut and mulberry trees; thistles and sorrel grew abundantly. Everywhere they looked, the Spaniards saw deer and rabbits and squirrels and more kinds of birds than they could keep track of. And, of course, there was good fishing in the river and sea. "The Río Guadalupe is a matter of wonder," wrote one crew member.

But Ayllón fell ill and died in the autumn of that year and without strong leadership, the men began to quarrel and fight. Many wandered into the back country and provoked the Indians, who struck back with a vengeance. Finally, with only 150 survivors of the original 500 men who had arrived just a few months earlier, the Spaniards returned to Hispaniola.

Francisco Chicora had gotten the best of Lucas Vázquez de Ayllón. By 1526, all that remained of the Spanish colony of Chicora were the tall tales of the charismatic Indian. Forty years would pass before any other Spaniards would attempt to settle along the Atlantic coast.

A typical sixteenth century sugar mill

Álvar Núñez Cabeza de Vaca

Explorer
*c.*1490–*c.*1560

". . . I overtook four of them [Spaniards] on horseback, who were astonished at the sight of me, so strangely habited as I was and in company with Indians. They stood staring at me a length of time, so confounded that they neither hailed me nor drew near to make an inquiry. . . ."[1]

So ended, in the spring of 1536, the astonishing journey of Álvar Núñez Cabeza de Vaca and his three companions. Over the course of eight years, since the day late in 1527 when half of the ill-fated Narváez expedition headed into the interior of Florida, the men had walked 6,000 miles—from the eastern Gulf Coast to the Pacific Ocean. The four survivors had lived among Indians, walking from village to village looking for food and shelter. As they walked for their very survival, they became the first Europeans to cross North America.

The Narváez expedition, made up of five ships and a crew of six hundred, had left Spain on June 17, 1527. The captain, Pánfilo de Narváez, was one of the sixteenth century's most notorious scoundrels. He was as cruel and stupid as Cabeza de Vaca, his "principal participant," was kind and thoughtful. Narváez, Cabeza later commented, could be counted on to make the wrong decision in almost any situation.

The five ships arrived at Hispaniola and from there headed to Cuba. Finally, in 1528, they set off for their destination, which was the Río de las Palmas in northern Mexico.

Bad storms blew the expedition off course, and it was April when the ships finally anchored off the west coast of Florida, near what is today St. Petersburg. At this point Narváez made the disastrous decision to divide into two groups—one, led by him and which included Cabeza de Vaca, was to travel overland, and the other would continue along the coast looking for a safe harbor. Many of Narváez's crew disagreed with the decision to leave the ships, but the captain would not change his mind.

Narváez began to tangle with the native Indians almost immediately. The Spanish soldiers wore armor and carried crossbows, and the captain was certain they could devastate any Indian attackers. What he did not reckon with was the skill and athletic ability of the Indians. To the amazement and terror of the Spanish, the Indians were excellent archers and so agile that they completely confounded the armed soldiers.

Finally, Narváez realized the overland journey was hopeless and sent a group to the coast to flag down the ships. The ships, the men reported back after several days, were nowhere to be found. (It was later learned that the ships, after searching the coast for Narváez and his men, had continued on across the Gulf to Mexico. They had, they found out years later, missed their leader's search party by only a few days.)

When the men realized they were stranded and completely surrounded by hostile Indians, they decided their only hope was to build boats themselves. The problem was that no one was a boatbuilder; only one, in fact, was even a carpenter. They had no tools, materials, or even food for themselves—nothing, except their horses and their own wits, which turned out to be as much as they needed.

In early autumn 1528, five boats carrying 245 men left what we now call St. Marks Bay. What a sight they must have been in boats that sat less than a foot above the ocean! Nearly a month later they anchored in Pensacola Bay. Shortly after arriving on land, they were greeted by an Indian attack.

The boats continued along the Gulf shore, crossing the mouth of the Mississippi. One boat capsized, then another; many of the crew members drowned, ran off into the woods, or were killed by Indians. Near Galveston Bay, Narváez dropped anchor but insisted on staying with his boat rather than venturing ashore. When a storm blew up, the boat broke loose of its mooring and was blown out to sea. The captain was never heard from again.

Alvar Nuñez Cabeza de Vaca crossing the Great American Desert

By the spring of 1529, the once mighty Narváez expedition of 600 men was down to four—Cabeza de Vaca, Castillo, Dorantes, and his black slave called Estevanico. In May, the four men left the island in Galveston Bay—a place they called Malhado ("bad luck") island—where they'd lived as slaves for the local Indians. They were a wretched sight. As Cabeza de Vaca later wrote, ". . . we escaped naked as we were born, with the loss of all we had . . . we looked like pictures of death."

From the site of Galveston, Texas, they headed west on foot. They walked literally for their lives. They survived by doing slave labor for the Indians and by convincing them that they were medicine men. In fact, they became widely known as high priests who, by saying prayers and gesturing, could cure anything. As they walked from village to village across the burning Texas plain, natives greeted them and took them to their homes to cure their sick.

They crossed the Colorado River near the site of Austin, Texas. Later they followed the Pecos River before veering west through southern New Mexico to present-day El Paso and into Sonora, Mexico. They crossed deserts and difficult mountains. They ate what nature offered them—walnuts, prickly pears, toads, snakes, and fish. When they found nothing, they starved. The four lived this way for eight years, walking across Texas, southern New Mexico, and into northern Mexico. The Indians were completely charmed by the big red-haired man, the tall black man, and the other two Spaniards. Hundreds of people followed as they walked to the Pacific Ocean. Finally, in 1536, eight years after their journey had begun, the weary walkers met up with their fellow Spaniards in Sonora, Mexico. They were then taken to Mexico City. Cabeza de Vaca departed shortly thereafter for Spain.

The story of the four survivors of the expedition of the long-lost Pánfilo de Narváez created a sensation in both Spain and Mexico. Cabeza de Vaca's journals, published in 1542, added greatly to the interest in the huge continent. Many in Spain began to wonder what exactly lay north of the vague borders of New Spain, or Mexico. When officials of the Spanish crown approached Cabeza about a return exploration, he respectfully declined.

Back home in Seville, Cabeza de Vaca could have lived on the glory of this accomplishment alone. But a few years later he was off again—this time to Brazil. He eventually became the governor of Paraguay, before being deposed by several men upset with Cabeza's intention of enforcing the strictest moral standards in the colony. He was sent home to Spain in chains and died in poverty a few years later. As often happens, it was only after his death that his accomplishments were recognized by his country and the world.

Cabeza de Vaca was the first person to mention buffalos. This engraving is from 1550.

Alonso Álvarez de Pineda
Explorer
(lifedates unknown)

Some Spanish explorers went looking for El Dorado, others for the Fountain of Youth; later many set off to find the Seven Cities of Cíbola. Alonso Álvarez de Pineda had a mission of mythical size, too, as he combed the coast of the Gulf of Mexico looking for a sea route to the Pacific Ocean. He was a skilled mariner who took his work very seriously, but in the end he was ashamed to have to report that the only interesting thing he'd seen had been the mouth of a huge river, which he named Río del Espíritu Santo (the river of the Holy Spirit). He was, in fact, the first European to see the Mississippi River.

Álvarez de Pineda was in command of an expedition organized by Francisco de Garay, the lieutenant governor of Jamaica. Garay was a rich man who longed to become even richer, and, so when the pilot Antón de Alaminos asked for his help in finding a route from the Gulf of Mexico to the Pacific, Garay quickly agreed.

The ships set off on their journey just before the end of 1518. They first landed on the west coast of Florida and immediately were attacked by Indians. Pineda escaped quickly and sailed west all the way to the Río Tampico in Mexico. On the way, as they sailed past the Mississippi's mouth, they noticed the huge volume of water pouring into the sea. They sailed upstream about twenty miles and anchored in the river for about a month.

They continued south along the coast of what is now Texas. In Mexico, near the mouth of the Pánuco River, they were attacked by Indians. All the fleet's ships but one were burned and many

Spaniards were killed—including Pineda. The remaining ship sailed on to Veracruz, and its crew told the Spaniards there the sad tale of Captain Pineda and the Garay expedition.

Pineda is not as well-known as many of the other Spanish explorers, but his accomplishments are still impressive. He not only discovered the Mississippi River, but he traded with the Indians along its mouth. Many, he reported wore gold ornaments. He and his crew members drew a map—The Pineda Chart of 1520—which shows correctly the main outlines of the Gulf of Mexico.

And, perhaps most importantly, as he was the first to sail completely around the western shores of the Gulf of Mexico, he was able to tell the world that, while there may be an El Dorado and a Fountain of Youth, there is no passage to the Pacific from the Gulf.

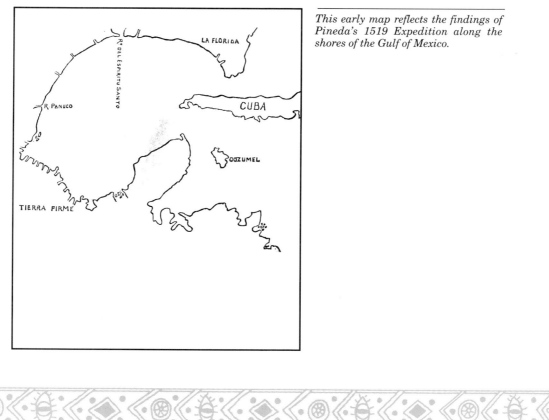

This early map reflects the findings of Pineda's 1519 Expedition along the shores of the Gulf of Mexico.

Hernando de Soto

Conquistador

*c.*1496, 1499, or 1500–1542

The news of Cabeza de Vaca's trek from the Gulf of Mexico to the Gulf of California sparked the imaginations—and the greed—of many conquistadors. In the mountain country, Cabeza's writings reported, there were signs of gold, silver, iron, and other valuable metals. For men such as Hernando de Soto, just a hint of riches was all they needed to begin planning their conquest.

De Soto had accompanied the ruthless conquistador Francisco Pizarro into Peru in the 1530s, and he returned to Spain a wealthy man. South America, the Spanish had learned, was full of riches, and the conquistadors had loaded their ships with as much gold and jewels as they would hold. The Spaniards had killed thousands of Indians and destroyed many temples in their conquest, but the ends, these soldiers seemed to believe, justified the means. According to Cabeza, North America might be another giant treasure chest just waiting to be opened.

De Soto decided he could make his mark—gaining both wealth and glory—in the region of the Gulf of Mexico. He imagined that Florida could become a seat of power such as Mexico or Peru. When the ambitious conquistador told Charles V of his plans for the western Gulf region, the Holy Roman Emperor and king of Spain granted him the right to settle there.

The eager conquistador bought seven ships with his own money and selected the most skilled crew he could find. He even asked Cabeza de Vaca to go along as guide but the experienced explorer, sensing something was wrong with de Soto's plan, decided not to go. In the settlement grant there was no mention of discovering natural resources or setting up new mines. How then would the settlement support itself? Cabeza de Vaca knew the answer. The greedy Spanish would steal anything and everything they could get their hands on.

The de Soto expedition arrived just north of the site of Fort Myers, Florida, on May 25, 1539. The captain wasted no time in applying the lessons he'd learned from Pizarro. He would enter an Indian village and take several hostages, including the chief. Then he'd demand food and lodging for his men. When he was ready to move on, they would take the hostages along, freeing them only when the next Indian village also agreed to their demands.

In this way, the Spaniards headed north to what is now Augusta, Georgia. They then traveled west into the Blue Ridge Mountains and south again to Mobile Bay before spending the winter of 1540–41 in Chickasaw Indian country in what today is the state of Mississippi.

Just below the site of Memphis, Tennessee, at the Chickasaw Bluffs, the expedition built four barges, and in May 1541, approximately two hundred and fifty men and about twenty horses were transported across the Mississippi River. The next few months were spent moving slowly among the Indian villages of northern Arkansas. The Spaniards found good supplies of maize and beans and dried fruits, but nothing that could be called treasure. By the end of the winter of 1542, de Soto decided to retreat to the Gulf.

Near the site of Natchez, Mississippi, the party stopped to scout for food. De Soto became very sick with a fever and died on May 21, 1542. His body was weighted with sand and dropped into the Mississippi River.

His successor wasted little time in moving the expedition west toward the Spanish settlement at Pánuco, Mexico. They crossed Louisiana and passed into Texas. After four months of traveling, they gave up this route and headed back toward the Mississippi. They would, their new captain decided, make the trip to New Spain by boat.

The sorry survivors of the de Soto expedition arrived in Mexico in the fall of 1543. They did not come with ships loaded with jewels and precious metals as they'd expected. They were starved and dressed in rags.

The de Soto expedition was a tragedy, both for the Spaniards and the Indians they treated so cruelly. The lessons learned, however, were valuable. De Soto failed because he was only interested in looting the country, not in settling it. This lesson was taken to heart by the next generation of Spaniards, who indeed came not just with the weapons of war but also with the tools of prosperity.

Hernando de Soto discovers the Mississippi River.

Fray Marcos de Niza

Explorer
? –1558

There was great excitement when word reached Mexico City late in 1538 that four survivors of the Narváez expedition had been found. The four—including Cabeza de Vaca and the black slave called Estevanico—hadn't been heard from for ten years, ever since their dastardly commander, Pánfilo de Narváez, had ordered half his expedition to leave their ships and explore the interior of Florida. The other men had all died of disease and starvation or were killed by the Indians.

The four castaways had lived with various Indian tribes and had walked across the continent, from the Gulf Coast to Texas and the Southwest and on to the Gulf of California. When the weary men were rescued, they told their fellow Spaniards all about the great empty lands they had traveled through.

Viceroy Antonio de Mendoza of New Spain (Mexico) decided to mount a new expedition to explore the northern lands. Cabeza de Vaca's official report gave just enough evidence of possible riches that many Spaniards were eager to conquer the "Northern Kingdom," as they called it. Mendoza signed on Estevanico, the black slave, to guide the explorers. He then chose a Franciscan friar Marcos de Niza, known as Fray Marcos, to serve as the official witness— in other words, the one who would report back to the eager Spaniards on all he saw and heard.

The friar, Estevanico, and several Indians set off from the province of New Galicia in northwest Mexico on March 7, 1539. Fray Marcos walked along in a gray robe cinched at the waist; Estevanico wore brightly colored robes, jingle bells at his wrists and ankles, and he carried a gourd rattle. Two sleek greyhounds walked at the black man's side.

The men spoke with Indians along their route and sent back messengers with news. The Indians all wear gold jewelry, the friar reported, and they speak of seven great cities somewhere to the north—cities full of gold and silver and turquoise.

Fray Marcos was sure the Indians were talking about the Seven Cities of Cíbola. According to Spanish legend, seven Portuguese bishops, fleeing an Arab invasion during the eighth century, sailed across the ocean and each founded a fabulous city. These cities were richer than anyone could imagine—richer even than Peru or Mexico. But where were these gold-lined cities?

Fray Marcos sent Estevanico and several Indian scouts ahead to find Cíbola's exact location. The black man had only been gone a few days before he sent a messenger back to the friar. Cíbola, it seemed, was only a month's journey ahead; Estevanico would try to get there with all speed.

Fray Marcos himself set off at once for Cíbola. He, too, passed through villages where he heard stories of these great cities. Cíbola, he was told, is not only full of gold but unicorns walk the streets!

Then one of Estevanico's messengers rushed toward Fray Marcos with terrible news. Estevanico and his scouts had reached Cíbola and had been killed by Indians.

Fray Marcos decided to press ahead anyway so he could at least look at the cities from a distance. Finally, near what today is the Zuñi Indian Reservation in New Mexico, the friar saw the first city of Cíbola, rising from a plain of brush. Beyond, he could see six other settlements all made of stone with terraces and flat roofs.

"The city of Cíbola," he wrote, "is larger than the city of Mexico

. . . the houses are of stone and lime and the portals and fronts are of turquoise."

The Spaniards were exuberant when the friar returned to New Spain with news of Cíbola. What they failed to note, however, was that even though the friar had seen the city, he hadn't seen the riches. The stories of turquoise and gold had come from the Indians, who seemed to understand both the Spaniard's love of fables and their love of gold.

Fray Marcos's expedition is remembered today not for any real contribution it made to the exploration of the lands north of Mexico but for the odd mixture of fact, fiction, and fantasy of the friar's own account. Many Spaniards were so eager to believe in these gold-filled cities that they signed up in great numbers for their country's next great journey north—the expedition of Francisco Vásquez de Coronado.

Estevanico

Francisco Vásquez de Coronado

Explorer

1510–1554

When Francisco Vásquez de Coronado was barely nineteen, a mystic from his native city of Salamanca, Spain, predicted three things would happen in Francisco's future: first, he would move very far away; next, he would become very powerful; and finally, he would have a bad fall from which he would never recover.

Ten years later, in 1539, Francisco was the governor of the far-off province of New Galicia in Mexico. And, his power and fame were soon to increase because he had just been chosen by King Philip II of Spain to lead that country's most ambitious expedition yet into the "Northern Kingdom."

The accounts of two earlier travelers, Cabeza de Vaca and Fray Marcos, had given Spain new hope that great riches lay just to the north of New Spain. After all, wasn't it said that the streets of the Indian cities were lined with gold and turquoise? Once the Indians were subdued—which of course, would be an easy matter for the well-armed Spanish—couldn't they then just help themselves to the treasure?

Fray Marcos himself joined the expedition to serve as guide. He would lead the group north from the Pacific coast town of Compostela, through what he'd earlier described as the "green valleys, passable trails, and over the one small hill, half a league long." This route would take them to Cíbola, "a city larger than the city of Mexico with great stone houses trimmed in turquoise."

On February 23, 1540, a great column of 230 cavalry soldiers, 32 infantry, 4 friars, 1 surgeon, 1,000 Indians, 1,000 horses, 600 mules, and an assortment of weapon and supply carriers left Compostela. They were led by a very confident General Coronado, who looked every inch the conqueror in his plumed helmet and full suit of golden armor.

Before long, however, the "green valleys and passable trails" became dangerously steep and rocky paths; the "one small hill" became the Sierra Madre Occidental Mountains. Several horses died of exhaustion as they carried men up and down the trails. As Coronado wrote, "All felt great anxiety and dismay to see that everything was the opposite of what Fray Marcos had told." Spirits were low as the horses crossed the border from Mexico into what today is the state of Arizona.

Finally, the expedition approached a wide valley where the earth looked pink and great mesas rose up on all sides. Deep in the valley, Coronado spotted a cluster of houses. At last, after seventy-seven days of hard travel, they had reached Cíbola.

A small party approached the stone and adobe pueblos to greet Cíbola's Zuñi Indians. The Spaniards were met by a hail of arrows.

General Vásquez de Coronado ordered an attack, and the large body of soldiers rushed at the Indian village, forcing the villagers to withdraw. The general himself was wounded twice before calm fell over the deserted city and the Spaniards were able to set up their headquarters.

Within a few days of arriving in the first of the Seven Cities of Cíbola, Coronado knew the terrible truth. There wasn't one that could really be called a city—they were simply villages. What's more, after thorough inspection, not a single house contained any silver or gold or even turquoise.

Coronado ordered Fray Marcos back to Mexico where he was promptly put in prison.

From Cíbola, Coronado sent out scouting parties to observe the surrounding area. Scouts came back with reports of more cities to the north (the Hopi pueblos) and a great river and canyon to the west (the Colorado River and the Grand Canyon.) Still others told of seeing a large river to the east (the Rio Grande) lined with many villages. The Indians there were friendly and generous, it was reported, and so Coronado decided to move his troops to the east for the winter, near the site of Albuquerque, New Mexico.

At the winter camp, Coronado spoke with an Indian, nicknamed the Turk, who was covered with gold jewelry. Where did this come from? the general asked, pointing to the gold. From the east, the Indian replied, from the buffalo plains.

General Coronado decided immediately that the Turk meant Quivira, the great city of Spanish legend. It was said that Quivira contained so much gold there weren't animals enough to haul it. The soldiers were all eager to journey farther east to find this great city, and so in the spring of 1541, the entire expedition left the mud houses of the Río Grande and headed into the "buffalo plains."

Finally, as spring turned to summer and Quivira remained always just past the horizon, Coronado ordered the more than 1,000 men and horses back to the winter camp on the Río Grande. Summer on the plains was harsh, but the general knew winter would be deadly and the expedition needed proper shelter.

Coronado himself and a number of scouts stayed on the plains to continue searching for Quivira. The soldiers traveled as far east as Kansas, where they stayed with the Wichita Indians. They asked the Wichita chiefs to lead them to Quivira, but the Indians had never heard of such a place.

Bitterly disappointed, Coronado ordered his scouts back to the Rio Grande, where they would spend the winter with the rest of the expedition. In the spring, he decided, they would all travel back to Compostela.

Just after Christmas 1541, General Coronado and two of his officers were exercising their horses along the riverbanks. They broke into a race, and the general quickly took the lead. Then, all of a sudden, his horse's saddle belt broke, and Coronado fell to the ground. The officers tried to rein in their own horses but couldn't, and Coronado was kicked in the head.

Just as the mystic of Salamanca had warned, the general never recovered. His spirits were broken both by his injury and by his failed expedition. "He is not the same man he was when your majesty appointed him to that governorship" wrote one official to King Philip II. Francisco Vásquez de Coronado lived out his days as an invalid and died in Mexico City on September 22, 1554.

General Coronado thought of himself as a failure, yet his discoveries were notable. His expedition reached the Río Grande, the Colorado River, the Grand Canyon, the Great Plains—he and his men, in fact, were the first Europeans to venture far into the interior of North America. Still, the one thing Coronado had hoped to find—gold—eluded them, and the brave general died feeling himself more the conquered than the conqueror.

Part Two

Early Hispanic America

The story of the conquistadors is a daring, ruthless one that has—as any good story must—a beginning and an end. These bold adventurers did not set out to settle the New World; they were really on get-rich-quick missions, searching desperately for gold and jewels. They came in a burst of glory, and blood, and then they were gone.

The settlement of America was bound to be less glamorous and to require very different kinds of adventurers. The conquistadors hadn't found any gold in North America, the way they had in Peru and Mexico. The fabled cities that Coronado searched for in Kansas remained just that—fables. To the next group of Spaniards would fall the task of finding the real treasures of America—the minerals, forests, soil, and other natural resources.

Some of the Spanish settlers, such as Father Junípero Serra, came for religious reasons. Others, such as Manuel Lisa, were forerunners of the modern entrepreneur, staring down risk and danger in the search for new markets. Still others were administrators, such as Diego de Vargas, who performed his job well but never disguised his longing to leave the land he called "remote beyond compare."

All the men in this section gave back to America as much as they took. They brought with them horses, cattle, pigs, plants, and farming tools, and they made dry, dusty land into fertile farms and ranches. They set high standards for building and architecture, so that the beauty of cities such as New Orleans and Santa Fe outshines that of most other American cities even today. Most of all, these settlers gave North America its Spanishness and ensured that Hispanic influence would become a lasting part of U.S. culture.

Pedro Menéndez de Avilés

Naval Officer, Founder of St. Augustine

1519–1574

". . . and as soon as the Indians saw him land, leaving their bows and arrows, they came to the said Adelantado and began to sing and to make gestures with their hands raised toward heaven, in manner of adoration, so that it was a wonderful thing to see. The Adelantado gave them many things and sweets to eat, which he had in one of the boats. . . . the Adelantado left them very happy and embarked on his ships and went sailing along the coast with his armada and discovered 8 leagues from there a good harbor, with a good beach, to which he gave the name of St. Augustine, because that was the first land he discovered in Florida, and he did so on the very day of St. Augustine [August 28, 1565]."[2]

From the account of Gonzalo Solís de Meras, brother-in-law of Pedro Menéndez and official recorder of the Menéndez Expedition

There was no question, Florida was a jewel that the Spanish wanted to own. Not only was it full of sweet-smelling, brilliantly colored flowers and trees, but—even more important to the power-hungry Spanish—its location was of vital strategic significance. All shipping from the West Indies, Peru, and New Spain (Mexico) had to enter the Straits of Florida from the west and sail to Cape Canaveral before riding the Gulf Stream east to Europe. Ever since Ponce de León landed on the peninsula in 1513, the Spanish believed Florida was rightfully theirs. So, when in 1565, King Philip II got word that a brave group of French Protestants, called Huguenots, was building a fort on the Atlantic coast, he was very concerned. He promptly chose one of his best naval officers, Pedro Menéndez de Avilés, to speed across the sea to stop them.

Captain Menéndez's naval career was already long and distinguished. He was well-known for bravely fighting pirates off the French coast. He was eager to serve his king in the New World and determined to carry out his orders with great energy and efficiency. By a contract signed in March 1565, Menéndez became *Adelantado* (governor) of Florida and was ordered to drive out, however he could, "settlers . . . of any other nations not subject to Us."

Captain Menéndez left Cádiz, Spain, in June. By late August, his fleet was on the Florida coast, as Solís reported, ". . . very much distressed, and in great suspense, not knowing whether the French were north or south. . . ." Finally, they spotted Indians on shore and, after determining that they were friendly, the Spaniards went ashore at what then became St. Augustine.

The Spaniards soon set off from St. Augustine and headed north, as directed by the Indians. Just off the mouth of the St. John's River, near present-day Jacksonville, the Spanish fleet skirmished with the forces of the French Huguenot leader, Jean Ribault. Menéndez's men fired into the French fleet and then headed for the safety of the harbor at St. Augustine, where on September 6, they began building a fort.

A week later Jean Ribault and his men were about to attack the new Spanish fort when they were driven south by a violent storm. Menéndez realized that, with the French forces shaken and disorganized, the time was right for an overland attack on the Huguenot's Fort Caroline, which had been left unprotected. The

Spaniards struck brutally, killing nearly all the fort's occupants, including women and children.

Captain Menéndez's fleet then returned to St. Augustine. The Spaniards soon became aware that members of Jean Ribault's hurricane-battered fleet were stranded in an inlet on the coast. They set out toward the French sailors and rescued them. Then, inexplicably, after Jean Ribault and his men begged for and were granted mercy, the Frenchmen were taken to shore and slaughtered. In a letter to Philip II, Menéndez explained that the killings were necessary "for the service of God Our Lord and of Your Majesty." Neither the government of France, nor history, was ever convinced such brutality had been necessary.

In fact, despite a distinguished, honorable career of service to the king of Spain, Pedro Menéndez de Avilés is probably best-remembered for his murder of the French Huguenots. Catherine de Médicis, mother of the ailing French king Charles IX, immediately sent a letter of strong protest to her son-in-law, King Philip II of Spain. She minced no words: ". . . I could not but feel an unbelievable heartache at the news that subjects of my son the king had been so foully slaughtered. . . . the Spanish ought to have been satisfied with taking them prisoner and then handing them over to my son the King. . . ." King Philip, however, never disputed that Captain Menéndez was indeed carrying out his wishes.

With the French settlers out of the way, Pedro Menéndez set about the job of firmly establishing Spain's control of Florida. He rebuilt Fort Caroline, renaming it San Mateo, and began a new fort in what is today South Carolina. Menéndez also traveled to Tampa Bay on Florida's west coast to establish a colony.

Pedro Menéndez, though, never stayed long at either St. Augustine or any of the other establishments, and this may have led to the downfall of all the Spanish settlements in Florida. Menéndez was an able administrator, but the men who served under him were not. Left alone, they fought among themselves and treated the Indians cruelly. As the Spanish should have learned from previous tries at settlement in America, the cooperation of local Indians tribes was vital.

Despite an energetic (and brutal) start, Spanish forts and settlements in Florida never prospered. By 1572, when King Philip called Captain Menéndez back to Spain for other duties, there were only seven married families living in St. Augustine and none in the forts further south.

Back in Spain in 1572, Pedro Menéndez asked King Philip for support in an all-out effort to colonize Florida. The captain wished permission to wage war against the Indians and then to bring in boatloads of Spanish families to set up households. The king was interested in this plan but first assigned Menéndez to duty in Europe with the Spanish Armada. In 1574, while once again serving his king, Pedro Menéndez de Avilés was killed.

As for St. Augustine, it floundered for many years after Menéndez's departure. Finally, in 1586, Spain's foothold in Florida was attacked and burned by England's Sir Francis Drake.

Juan de Oñate

Colonist

1550?–1630

Despite the earlier efforts of Fray Marcos, Estevanico, and Coronado, as the sixteenth century drew to a close, New Mexico was, as the Spanish viewed it, still largely unsettled and, "uncivilized." What's more, authorities in Spain and New Spain (Mexico) seemed more unwilling than ever to send men and equipment into the northern lands. The earlier expeditions had given little hope that there was much to gain from seizing Indian lands in what today is New Mexico and Arizona. Despite rumors of huge stores of gold and silver, all who'd traveled to these remote regions had returned—if they returned at all—empty-handed.

In 1595, however, Juan de Oñate, the son of a wealthy Spanish pioneer in Mexico, received permission to outfit an expedition that would travel into the "Northern Kingdom." His goals were twofold—to establish a colony and to convert the Indians to Christianity.

Three years later, in January 1598, 400 men, many of whom brought wives and children, and 7,000 head of cattle began the slow journey up the Río Grande. By April, they were within twenty-five miles of present-day El Paso, Texas. Within a few weeks they had crossed into New Mexico.

Oñate and an advance group of soldiers visited several Indian villages before deciding to move the expedition to San Juan, today called Española. On July 11, 1598, Oñate proclaimed this village, which he called San Juan de los Caballeros, the first Spanish settlement in New Mexico. By August, the foundation for a church was laid. Shortly afterwards, the Spaniards built a second settlement on the west side of the Rio Grande and named it San Gabriel.

Unfortunately, these Spaniards—just like the many who'd preceded them into North America—chose to spend more time searching for gold than working the land. When the settlers realized there was no gold or silver or turquoise waiting to be plucked from the soil, they became restless. Many wanted to return to Mexico.

Oñate would not let the settlers leave, and his strict discipline soon made him an unpopular leader. As for the Indians, they resented the Spanish intrusion on their lands. They resented, too, the white man's religion, which the Franciscan friars tried to force upon them with a heavy hand.

Finally, hostilities between the Spaniards and the Pueblos were brought to a head near Acoma. Some Spanish soldiers, thinking the Indians intended to give them fresh supplies, climbed up the high walls of the Pueblos' "sky village." There, the trapped Spaniards were attacked and killed. The group's leader had been Oñate's own nephew, Juan de Zaldivar.

Oñate was so upset at the news of the massacre that he ordered his soldiers to strike back. The well-armed Spaniards outnumbered the Indians, and, after several days of fierce fighting, they had killed nearly 800 Pueblos. Many more, including women and children, were taken prisoner and treated very harshly.

The viceroy in New Spain rewarded Oñate by sending him fresh recruits and supplies. Finally, Oñate could turn his attention away from the settlement and begin his exploration of the territory. In 1601, he and eighty soldiers explored the land east and west of the settlement, going all the way to the Colorado River and the Gulf of California.

When Oñate returned to San Gabriel, the colony was nearly deserted. The settlers, it seemed, had tired of the hard life, strict discipline, and escaped down the Rio Grande. All that remained of Spanish New Mexico were a few friars and Oñate's exploring party.

As the refugees from San Gabriel returned to New Spain, the authorities began to question Oñate's word on several matters. Captain Oñate hadn't told them there was no gold or silver; he hadn't mentioned the fierce battles with the Pueblos. Finally, in 1604, Oñate was forced to resign his positions of governor and captain general of New Mexico.

He returned to Mexico City in disgrace and nearly penniless. Just like Coronado before him, he had spent his entire fortune trying to find wealth in the province of New Mexico. And, like the earlier explorer, he never recovered from his failure.

The Pueblo of Taos

Gaspar Pérez de Villagrá

Colonist, Poet

1558–?

One of Juan de Oñate's young captains—Gaspar Pérez de Villagrá—had a passion for poetry and a flair for history.

In 1610, some twenty years after accompanying Oñate on the slow journey up the Rio Grande to New Mexico's first settlement at San Juan Pueblo, Villagrá published his *Historia de la Nuevo Mexico*. He thus became America's first epic poet.

Captain Pérez de Villagrá was a very well-educated soldier. He graduated from Spain's University of Salamanca in 1580 and then spent seven years as an adviser at the Court of Philip II in Madrid. But, as with many young Spaniards of his day, he was hungry for adventure and so quickly grabbed the chance to sail for New Spain and to join in Oñate's efforts to colonize New Mexico.

Villagrá's *Historia de la Nuevo Mexico* helped Spaniards understand the difficulties faced by colonists. The land, they learned from his epic, was desolate and the Indians hostile. Despite Villagrá's own brushes with death, he sympathized with the American natives' sorrow at losing their culture and religion to the European invaders.

In the following excerpt from his poem, Villagrá has barely escaped an Indian trap set for him near the pueblo at Acoma. He is near starvation and has killed his beloved dog for its meat. As the dog is dying, the soldier decides he can't eat his pet's meat.

He is ready to accept that his luck has simply run out.

In downcast mood I now took up my journey,
Leaving the poor dog dead. Sad fate beset me,
Till I descried a towering cliff uprising,
Beneath which flowed a stream of purest crystal.
Blinded and burnt with thirst, into its waters
I threw myself, and drank. This quenched my burning.
A bit of corn I spied, dropped there by someone;
At this, I knelt, and thanked the God Almighty
For this most timely aid. Then, on earth crawling,
Gathered a handful of the corn and ate it.
By rest and food refreshed, I then proceeded,
Seeking the city by our leader founded,
His capital, San Juan. Now fortune favored.
Starting upon my way, I soon encountered
Three of our men, out searching for their horses

. . . .

They called, demanding who I was; I answered,
And, at my name, their joy was so tremendous
That, in delight, they fired their arquebuses.
Heaven-sent impulses! For it chanced the Indians
Following me, were closing in for capture.
Hearing the guns, they turned and fled, believing
That the whole Spanish army lay before them[3]

. . . .

The Missions of New Mexico
and the Pueblo Revolt of 1680

Much as Spain's King Philip III might have wanted to give up on New Mexico after Juan de Oñate's failure as governor, he found he couldn't. The Franciscan friars had converted thousands of Indians, and abandoning these new Christians was now unthinkable. And so, in 1609 New Mexico was made a royal colony, directly under the king's rule.

The new royal governor, Pedro de Peralta, promptly moved the colony's capital from San Gabriel to a new village called Santa Fe. The Spanish then set themselves to the task of converting as many more Indians as they could. In fact, they didn't stop at changing the Indian's religion; they tried to remake the natives into proper Spaniards. It was an effort that was doomed from the start.

Daily contact between the Indians and their Spanish rulers came at the missions, which were communities of Indians led by one or more priests. Mission churches were built as close to the center of an already existing Indian village as possible. The church was always the highest, most imposing building. So, too, the word of the priest was of supreme importance and not to be challenged. (If the Indians did decide to resist the church's authority, soldiers were stationed at all missions.)

What the Spanish never thought to consider though was that the Indians already had both their own culture and religion, and these meant as much to them as Christianity did to the Spanish. The Franciscan friars expected the Indians to live, work, even dress like Spaniards. They outlawed all Indian songs, dances, and religious symbols. After a time, the Spaniards convinced themselves the

Indians had forgotten their religion; in fact, they'd only pushed it into hiding.

When toward the mid-1650s the Indians were faced with epidemics of small pox and measles and later, after a long drought, with starvation, they began to rebel against Spanish rule. Many Indians were sure Pueblo rain dances and chants would help their crops, and that their own medicine men could fight sickness just as well as the Spanish doctors. The independent spirit of the Pueblo Indians finally was forced out of hiding, and tribal leaders began to organize what became the Pueblo Revolt of 1680.

The revolt was planned in complete secret for months before its scheduled date of August 11, 1680. To let all Indians know the planned date, runners carried knotted yucca cords from one village to another. One knot was untied each new day, and the number of knots left told how many days until the revolt would begin.

On August 9, two runners were captured by the Spanish. When the Pueblos learned that the Spanish had uncovered the plan, they decided to attack the very next day—August 10.

The revolt was swift and brutal. Many Spaniards in settlements throughout New Mexico were killed. Finally, on August 22, after nearly two weeks of battle, the royal governor, Antonio de Otermín, surrendered in Santa Fe. The stunned colonists left their homes and began the long walk south. The Indians watched, feeling that as long as the Spanish were out of New Mexico, it didn't matter whether they were dead or alive.

The Spanish resettled in El Paso, knowing someday—but when?—they would attempt to recapture New Mexico. In the meantime, they would have to live with the shame of being the only Europeans ever ousted by Indians from a New World colony.

Diego de Vargas
Governor of New Mexico
1643–1704

More than ten years after the Pueblo Revolt of 1680 ousted the Spanish from New Mexico, a nobleman from Madrid decided to spend his own money to win the colony back. "I faced, overcame, and conquered all this at my own expense," the governor wrote to an officer of King Carlos in 1696. ". . . [T]he greater the risks and obstacles, the more my spirit was kindled, moving me to carry out the conquest. . . ."

Indeed there were many risks, financial and otherwise. The Indians were not eager to be under the thumb of the Spanish once again and fought hard to preserve their independence. Also, New Mexico's natural resources were poor and supporting the struggling colony was expensive. Many in Spain and New Spain (Mexico) were beginning to grumble that the colony in New Mexico took money away from the more valuable settlements on the Pacific Coast and in Texas.

Why would someone like Diego de Vargas take on such a responsibility? Mainly for money. His family owned farms and vineyards in Spain and his family was often in debt. His letters home are full of advice about legal and business matters and about how to settle family squabbles—mostly about money. He was terribly homesick in New Mexico, but, as he wrote in one letter, he hoped to earn enough money from his long stay to give loved ones security for their entire lives: ". . . I contemplate the comfort of having my heart's treasures, my beloved children, protected. . . . Out of such consideration, I could have done no more than to have exiled myself to this kingdom, at the ends of the earth and remote beyond compare."

Despite the hardships, however, Governor de Vargas was able to enjoy a long, productive term in office. He sent missionaries to live among the Indians; he recruited families from New Spain to settle his colony, families whose descendants still live in New Mexico. He made sure that Spain would continue governing New Mexico for many years to come.

Governor Diego de Vargas hoped to return to Madrid to spend his last years with his children and grandchildren, but he never returned to Europe. He died in April 1704, at the age of sixty, following a skirmish with Apache Indians near Bernalillo, New Mexico. He was quietly buried in Sante Fe, thousands of miles from his homeland.

An early view of Santa Fe

Joseph Azlor Vitro de Vera, the Marqués de Aguayo

Defender of Texas

?–1723?

Until the beginning of the 1700s, only the Indians and the Spanish seemed to care much about the southwestern part of the American continent. In 1719, however, when France and Spain were at war in Europe, the two nations began to argue over their lands on this continent, too. The French decided the Spanish province of Texas, which was so close to France's Louisiana, was worth a fight. The proud Spaniards vowed not to lose an inch of Texas soil and assigned one of their ablest leaders in Mexico—Joseph Azlor Vitro de Vera, the Marqués de Aguayo—to raise a small army and head for San Antonio.

The French governor in Louisiana made the first move. In June 1719, he instructed an "army" of seven soldiers to take over the eastern Texas mission of San Miguel de los Adaes. The French did this swiftly and efficiently—helped by the fact that the one Franciscan friar and one Spanish soldier stationed at the mission were away at the time. The "attack" nevertheless greatly worried the Spanish, especially because rumor had it that the French wanted to push them all the way back to the Rio Grande—in other words, completely out of the huge province.

Aguayo was the right man to defend Spain from such a humiliating defeat. He was a well-educated nobleman of unquestioned loyalty to the Spanish Crown. He was also very wealthy and willing to use his own fortune when necessary to outfit his army. He arrived at the garrison at San Antonio in the late summer of 1720 and began recruiting soldiers and preparing for the expedition.

By October, the army of 500 was ready to head north. Aguayo's instructions to them were clear: They would stop at nothing less than complete control of the province, including all former Spanish missions and occupation of the Bay of Espíritu Santo at the mouth of the Guadalupe River, north of present-day Corpus Christi.

The Marqués de Aguayo and his army proceeded north from San Antonio. They crossed first the Guadalupe River, then the San Marcos and Colorado rivers before summer began. By July, they finally made it past the rain-swollen Trinity River and were able to travel more quickly toward the Spanish mission of San Francisco de los Tejas, which had been established four years earlier just west of the Neches River. On the banks of the Neches, Aguayo met up with Saint-Denis, a Frenchman, who, because of his love for the daughter of a Spanish captain, had begun passing secrets to his country's enemy. (Actually, he was a double-agent, taking Spanish secrets back to the French. This wasn't learned until several years later.) Saint-Denis told Aguayo that France and Spain were no longer at war, and, so, there was no reason to go any farther than the spot where they stood.

Aguayo, however, was determined to cross the Neches and reach the site of the Mission San Miguel, a few miles west of Louisiana's Natchitoches. There he planned to establish a presidio, or fort, which would serve the Spanish should they again find themselves at war with the French.

Saint-Denis tried to convince the marqués that the presidio was no longer necessary, but Aguayo would not be talked out of his plan. Nor would he pay attention to the threats received from the French in Louisiana. He proceeded on to the mission, between the Sabine and Red rivers, several miles east of Natchitoches, and, in two months his men completed the presidio.

With the work done to this satisfaction, he returned with his soldiers to San Antonio. There, in the spring of 1722, his men completed that settlement's presidio. Then the marqués and a few of his soldiers—many stayed in San Antonio to man the new fort —headed toward the Rio Grande. It was nearly winter, and the weary nobleman felt it was time to retire to the warmth of Mexico.

What did the Marqués de Aguayo's three years of service in Texas amount to? When he finally crossed the Rio Grande and headed into Mexico, he left behind ten missions, where before there had been seven, four military presidios where there had been two, two hundred and seventy soldiers instead of seventy, and two forts built for the sole purpose of heading off a foreign attack—Los Adaes and Espíritu Santo. Texas was now truly a Spanish stronghold. The hold, in fact, was strong enough to last 115 years.

San Antonio River

Father Junípero Serra

Founder of the California Missions

1713–1784

Miguel José Serra could have lived a happy, carefree life on the beautiful Mediterranean island of Majorca, where he was born in 1713. His childhood was full of sunshine and the sound of bells ringing in the tall church tower. Boys of Majorca, however, just like those on the Spanish mainland, loved to tell adventure stories about the New World. Miguel José made up such stories, too, about walking across the harsh country to live among Indians. The other boys always liked Miguel's stories best; they always seemed so true to life.

Miguel was a brilliant student who went on to the university in Palma, Majorca's capital city. When he wasn't deep in his religious studies, he visited the Church of San Francisco, named for Saint Francis of Assisi, who devoted his entire life to helping the poor. Miguel decided he, too, wanted to join the Order of Saint Francis, and so when he finished his university studies at sixteen he joined the order. He then took the name Junípero, after one of Saint Francis's most devoted followers.

Father Junípero Serra never forgot his boyhood stories of the New World and in 1749—after many years of teaching at the University in Palma—he decided to go to Mexico to work among the Indians there. The sea voyage from Spain to Mexico lasted nearly

100 days. When the ship arrived in Mexico's port of Veracruz, nearly all the crew and passengers were ill from lack of food and water. Father Serra, however, did not want to waste time resting. He and the two priests who had come with him set off at once for their new home at the College of San Fernando in Mexico City.

The walk was long and difficult over rough rocky terrain. One night an insect bit Junípero in the leg while he slept. The next morning his foot and leg were badly swollen, but he refused treatment. The infection never healed, and the pain lasted Junípero's entire life.

Once in Mexico City, Father Serra began his work among the Indians of New Spain and Baja—or Lower—California. He criss-crossed Mexico on foot, visiting missions and teaching the Indians about Christianity. In 1767, Father Serra became head of all the missions in Baja California.

Then, later that year, the Spanish king and the foreign minister, José Gálvez, decided it was time to establish missions farther north, in Alta California—what we know as the state of California. It seems Spain was beginning to worry that either Russia or Great Britain might try to colonize Alta California if Spain didn't make her mark there first.

Gálvez chose Father Serra to oversee the establishment of these new missions. He then named Gaspar de Portolá to be Governor of both Baja and Alta California and head of the expedition. Gálvez and Portolá decided that one mission should be located in San Diego, another near the port at Monterey, and a third somewhere in between. The Spanish had never undertaken a land expedition into Alta California before but they knew about San Diego and Monterey from the expeditions of earlier Spanish and Portuguese seamen. Two Spaniards had inspected Monterey's port and the most famous among them—Sebastián Vizcaíno—had described it as a perfect harbor.

Father Serra traveled by land from the interior of Mexico to San Diego. The journey was slow, and Father Serra's leg caused him great pain. The expedition was overjoyed when, on July 1, 1769, they all stood on top of a hill and saw San Diego Bay below— "beautiful to behold," in the words of Father Serra. There, anchored in the bay, were the two Spanish supply ships, the *San Antonio* and the *San Carlos*. Their joy turned to sadness, however, when they learned that many of the ships's sailors had died of scurvy —a disease we now know to be caused by a lack of fresh fruits and vegetables.

Governor Portolá sent the *San Antonio* back to Baja California to pick up medicine, supplies, and a new crew. In the meantime, he decided to begin the overland expedition to Monterey Bay. Portolá hoped that when the land expedition found Monterey, the second ship, the *San Carlo*, which would have shadowed the Portolá's men up the coast, would already be waiting in the harbor with food and supplies.

Father Serra was too weary to accompany Governor Portolá on his long walk to Monterey. Instead he immediately began scouting the location for their first mission, the Mission of San Diego. On July 16, 1769, a cross was raised at the site, and a chapel was built from tree branches. A few frightened Indians approached, looked over the small hut, and left.

One quiet day shortly afterward, when most of the soldiers were on board the ship and only Father Serra and a few others were in the chapel, the Indians returned and began shooting arrows at the chapel. The soldiers who were on shore quickly opened fire with their guns and managed to chase the Indians away. The Indians came back though, when Father Serra offered to have the Spanish doctor treat the wounded. It was the beginning of a kind of truce between the two sides.

Inside an early mission

Several months later, on January 24, 1770, Governor Portolá and his men returned from the north. The overland expedition had been a failure. For weeks the men had trudged over inhospitable terrain, looking for Monterey Bay but never finding it. Portolá sent some scouts who came back with word of a huge arm of the ocean which they named "San Francisco," after Saint Francis. But no perfect harbor, no Monterey.

Governor Portolá was discouraged with the expedition's progress. Many sailors had died of scurvy, the Indians were armed, and Portolá himself could not find Monterey Bay by land. And, to make matters worse, the supply ship, *San Antonio*, had not yet returned to San Diego. We simply cannot go on, Portolá announced, we must return to Baja.

Father Serra was terribly disappointed and managed to convince Portolá to wait a few weeks more—until after the feast of Saint Joseph on March 19. Finally, on the morning of March 19, the governor ordered his men to prepare the ships to return to Mexico the next morning.

Junípero decided to take a last evening walk along the shore. At sunset a thick fog lifted for the first time all day. Father Serra looked out at the sea, and, there, just at the mouth of the bay, he saw the sails of the *San Antonio* shining bright in the sun.

Portolá immediately called off the return trip and made plans for the second overland expedition to find Monterey. The *San Antonio*, with Father Serra aboard, shadowed the expedition up the coast. The voyage from San Diego to Monterey took forty-six days. The bay was wide and beautiful, just as Vizcaíno had described 120 years before. But it was not sheltered and really not a proper harbor at all. The crafty old sailor, it seems, had told Spanish officials what they wanted to hear, not what he'd actually seen.

Father Serra went ashore and oversaw the building of the second mission. On June 3, 1770, Father Serra held services in the new chapel. The soldiers shot their guns in the air. Governor Portolá took possession of the land for the King Charles III and cast handfuls of grass and stone to the four winds.

Soon afterwards Governor Portolá returned to Mexico—his work in California was over. Nearly sixty years old, Father Serra's work was just beginning. He and his fellow Franciscans soon founded a third mission, in a beautiful valley just east of Monterey at the mouth of the Carmel River. He loved this site so much that he made the Mission San Carlos his permanent home.

By 1774, Father Serra had founded five missions along a road that later became known as El Camino Real—the King's Highway —which connected the sites. The old priest walked the road, never tiring of the lovely flowers and twisted wisteria.

By the end of his life, he'd established nine missions, whose names are still familiar to us today—Mission Dolores at San Diego, San Luis Obispo, San Juan Capistrano. In these missions, Indians from various California tribes lived and worked. They raised food, worked at a trade, wove cloth from wool, and made wine from grapes.

Father Serra visited each of the missions often, but he always returned to his home at Carmel. It was there he died on August 28, 1784. The bells from the towers of all the missions—from San Diego to San Francisco—rang out to mark the end of Junípero's long, productive life.

Gaspar de Portolá and the Search for Monterey

While Father Serra was busy settling California's first mission at San Diego in July 1769, Governor Gaspar de Portolá and his men headed north to find an overland route to Monterey. The Bay of Monterey had first been spotted more than 160 years earlier by an explorer named Sebastián Vizcaíno. He'd reported finding a beautiful, nearly perfect harbor, which he named after Viceroy Monterey of New Spain.

By the middle of September, Governor Portolá's men had reached some very high mountains—the Santa Lucía Range in what we now call the Big Sur region. The Spanish had heard of this range, and they believed Monterey lay just on the other side. Day by day they climbed through narrow gorges and near precipes that were, as Friar Juan Crespi said, "capable of frightening even the wild animals that lived there."

When they reached the other side of the mountains, they heard the ocean but couldn't see the shore. Portolá sent out a group of scouts, and they returned with bad news: While they could find many of the landmarks mentioned on the old Spanish maps, nowhere did they see the protected bay of Monterey.

Where was Monterey? They had plotted the latitude and longitude as marked by the earlier explorers but still found nothing to match their descriptions. Were their navigational tools so far off? Some, like the cosmographer Miguel Costanzo, began to believe that "we might have left behind us the port we were seeking, by reason of the great circuit we had made in passing through the mountain range."

Finally, Governor Portolá gathered his officers and the two friars, and they discussed what their next move should be. As Costanzo wrote:

> He drew attention to the scarcity of provisions that confronted us; to the large number of sick we had amoung us (there were seventeen men crippled and unfit for work); to the season already far advanced; and to the great sufferings of those who remained well. . . . All the men voted unanimously that the journey be continued [north] as this was the only course that remained, for we hoped to find—through the grace of God—the much desired port of Monterey. . . . [4]

When Governor Portolá ordered a scouting party to hunt desperately for the best route to Monterey Bay, Friar Juan Crespi and Costanzo went along. They, therefore, were among the first white men to see San Francisco Bay. The sight didn't overjoy them, however —they were not too disappointed that they were looking at the now-fabled Monterey.

Entrance to the Golden Gate

October 31, 1769. . . . As soon as we ascended to the summit we descried a great bay formed by a point of land which runs far out into the open sea and looks like an island. Farther out . . . six or seven white *farallones* [rocky islands] of different sizes were to be seen. . . . In view of these signs. . . . we came to the recognition of this port; it is that of Our Father San Francisco, and we have left that of Monterey behind.[5] —Father Crespi

Many tried to believe this was Monterey, but Portolá knew better. They explored all along what we now call the Golden Gate, and then, bitterly disappointed, they turned south again.

December 5, 1769: "We did not know what to think of the situation. A port so famous as that of Monterey, so celebrated, and so talked of in its time by energetic, skillful, and intelligent men, expert sailors . . . is it possible to say that it has not been found after the most careful and earnest effort, carried out at the cost of so much toil and fatigue?

. . . on the return [of the scouting party] from the examination of the mountain range, our commander laid before his officers the unhappy plight in which we were placed—without provisions other than sixteen sacks of flour, without hope of finding the port and consequently of finding the ship which might aid us. . . .

The commander himself resolved on the return [to San Diego]— in view of the few provisions that remained, the excessive cold, and, above all, the snow that was beginning to cover the mountain range . . . believing that if the passage over the mountains became impossible, we should all perish."[6] —Miguel Costanzo

They headed back to San Diego and, after very nearly starving, arrived at San Diego on January 24, 1770. In the words of Governor Portolá they gave "thanks to God that, notwithstanding the great labors and privations we had undergone, not a single man had perished. . . ."

Later that year, with the supply ship *San Antonio* shadowing the overland expedition, Governor Portolá made another try.

On May 31, Father Crespi, who had made the land trek with Portolá, spotted the *San Antonio* in Monterey Bay. "It saluted us with cannon shots to let us know that it recognized us, and then came in to the very spot where our cross was."

Why hadn't Governor Portolá's expedition been able to find Monterey the first time? For several reasons: First, the view from land was very different from the view at sea. Also, and this may be the most important reason, the harbor at Monterey had become part of Spanish mythology. In other words, the more it was talked of, the more "perfect" it became until no real harbor could compare. The Spaniards were, in fact, looking for something almost entirely made up.

But now, at last, they'd found the real Monterey. In a glorious ceremony, they took possession of it in the name of King Charles III of Spain. As Father Junípero Serra wrote:

> . . . And thus, after raising aloft the standard of the King of Heaven, we unfurled the flag of our Catholic Monarch likewise. As we raised each one of them, we shouted at the top of our voices: "Long live the Faith! Long live the King!" All the time the bells were ringing, and our rifles were being fired, and from the boat came the thunder of big guns.[7]

Andrés Almonaster y Rojas (1725–1798)
and
the Baroness de Pontalba (1795–1874)
New Orleans's Spanish Benefactors

When France secretly handed New Orleans over to Spain in 1762, it gave away the sea outlet for half a continent. Despite the city's location, many Spaniards turned their noses up at the very idea of living in this town of dirty, dusty streets and shabby wooden buildings. It wasn't until one Spaniard, Andrés Almonaster y Rojas, decided to use his own fortune to rebuild New Orleans, that it became the elegant city we know today.

Almonaster was a shipping merchant and entrepreneur, and he made it clear early on that he was willing to invest in New Orleans. In 1779, a hurricane tore through the city, destroying the Charity Hospital, which had been built in 1736. Andrés spent $100,000 of his own money to replace the old hospital with a far greater structure.

Then, on March 21, 1788—Good Friday that year—a candle on a private altar on Chartres Street tipped over and started a great fire. Because it was such a solemn religious day, the city's churches refused to ring their bells in alarm. The winds were high, and within five hours between 800 and 900 buildings were destroyed.

The loss was devastating and, to make matters worse, no public money was available to rebuild the hospitals, churches, and government buildings that had been destroyed. Almonaster again came forward and paid for much of the rebuilding himself.

First, he replaced the St. Louis Cathedral with a far lovelier building. The new cathedral, facing the Place d'Armes—now called

Jackson Square—became New Orleans's most imposing landmark. In addition, he provided for a new municipal building, which became known as the Cabildo, the name of the governing body whose home it was. Almonaster also used his influence to rebuild the old French Market.

Pontalba Buildings

New Orleans officials took steps to prevent any more disastrous fires. They divided the town into four districts and organized a volunteer fire department, but even these preparations weren't enough. In December 1794, another terrible fire destroyed more than 200 buildings. All the structures were in the shopping district, and, when the blaze was brought under control, only two stores were still standing.

Again, Almonaster stepped forward and built a new customs house —and, as before, the new building was far grander than the original one. Gradually, through years of fires and rebuilding, the makeshift wooden structures of the old French city were replaced by the stone, brick, and stucco ones favored by the Spanish. New Orleans began to take on a distinctive Spanish look with its ornate iron balconies, shuttered windows, and stuccoed walls. This style suited the hot, humid climate of the Mississippi Delta.

In the 1850s, long after Don Almonaster's death in 1798, his daughter Michaela, the Baroness de Pontalba, undertook her own building project. She completed New Orleans's most elegant collection of townhouse apartments—the Pontalba Buildings—which still grace Jackson Square. Medallions at regular spaces along the beautiful iron-railed balconies feature the initials of the two prominent families—A and P for Almonaster and Pontalba—and remind visitors of the influence of New Orleans's Spanish benefactors.

The Lópezes and the Riveras
of Newport
Colonial Merchants

Queen Isabella I of Spain had a lot on her mind in 1492. Not only was she anxious about the Italian mariner, Christopher Columbus, and his voyage into the unknown, but she needed to settle the question of Spain's Jews. Catholic church leaders were urging her to make the Jews either convert to Christianity or leave the country, and the queen finally went along. The result was the infamous Spanish Inquisition, which forced hundreds of thousands of Jews to flee, first to neighboring Portugal and then—when the Portuguese began their own Inquisition—to friendlier countries such as Holland or England. By the 1700s, many Spanish-Portuguese, or Sephardic, Jewish families— such as the Lopezes and the Riveras—were on their way to colonial America. In America, they hoped that they could reclaim the religion Queen Isabella had taken away nearly 300 years earlier.

Jacob Rodríquez Rivera (1719–1789) and Aarón López (1731– 1782) were cousins. The Riveras had moved to New York from Spain during the early eighteenth century; the Lópezes came from Portugal shortly after. In their homelands, they lived openly as Christians but secretly as Jews. In New York, they practiced Judaism openly in a congregation with other Sephardics.

After several years in New York, a group of Sephardic families began discussing the idea of moving to the small community of Newport, Rhode Island. Newport, they'd heard, was an excellent place to do business. Its port was better than Boston's, and its climate milder. And, even more important than the business prospects, Rhode Island was a colony founded on the principle of religious freedom.

In New York, Jacob Rodríquez Rivera had established a highly successful industry—making candles from the waxy substance that could be separated from the oil of the sperm whale. The spermaceti industry grew rapidly after Rivera set up his business in Newport in the 1740s. It was so successful, in fact, that by 1750 he asked his cousin Aaron, who clearly had a flair for commerce, to leave New York and join him in Newport.

Aarón López was twenty-one when he arrived in Newport in 1752. He began work as a shopkeeper but quickly became involved with every aspect of international trade. He not only shipped his cousin's whale-oil products, but began bringing in loads of rum, sugar, chocolate, and molasses from Europe, the West Indies, and Africa. Within ten years of his first day in Newport, Aarón was one of the wealthiest men in Rhode Island.

Aarón López

Jacob Rodríquez Rivera

By the early 1760s, the Sephardic families of Newport decided to build a temple where their congregation could worship. They received generous contributions from their old congregation in New York and hired a well-known architect, Peter Harrison, to design the building. The Touro Synagogue—as it was later named—was consecrated in 1763, making it the first synagogue established in America. It was, and is, considered a place of quiet grace and beauty.

As the 1770s began, Aarón López and Jacob Rodríquez Rivera were involved in the full range of shipping interests, including one of the most tragic—slavery. Ships owned by the two families would sail to the west coast of Africa carrying a cargo of New England rum. In Africa, the rum would be traded for slaves, who would then be taken to the West Indies. Once in the Caribbean, yet a third trade would be made—slaves for sugar, which would then be shipped back to Newport. For these wealthy merchants, the slave trade, unfortunately, seemed to be "just another business."

The coming of the American Revolution, however, signaled an end to business as usual in Newport. By 1775, with the British blockading Newport harbor, López and Rivera decided the town was just too dangerous for their families, and they prepared to move. (Moving the López family was no small job: Aarón's first wife had died in 1762, leaving him with seven children. He later married Rivera's daughter, Sally, and the two had ten more.)

Aarón López resettled his family in Leicester, Massachusetts, and tried to save whatever he could of his business. Jacob Rivera joined him a short while later. Once again, López became active in the community and was widely admired as a patron of the arts and education.

In May 1782, López and his wife and children set out from Leicester on a trip to Providence and Newport to visit friends. Sally

López and the children rode in carriages but Aarón López, as was his custom, rode alone with a servant in a sulky. Near Providence, Aarón stopped to let his horse drink from a pond. The horse moved forward into the pond and pitched the sulky into the water. For all Aarón López's accomplishments, he had never learned to swim, and he drowned before his servant could save him.

Aarón López's funeral was held at the Touro Synagogue and was attended by the leading dignitaries of the day. The eulogy was delivered by Ezra Stiles, president of Yale College. López was praised for his integrity and generosity. As President Stiles said, "for honor and extent of commerce probably surpassed by no merchant in America."

Newport's leading shipping merchant was buried in the Jewish cemetery there, not far from the famous synagogue he'd helped found. Jacob Rodríquez Rivera, who died in 1789, lies nearby.

Touro Synagogue

Bernardo de Gálvez

Governor of Louisiana

1746–1786

While George Washington and the Continental army fought against the British along the eastern seaboard, an American and a Spanish aristocrat met in New Orleans to decide the best way to get the British out of the Lower Mississippi. The American was Oliver Pollock, and the Spaniard was Bernardo de Gálvez, who in 1777 had become governor of the Spanish province of Louisiana. The two men were very different but they were united in their hatred for the British.

Oliver Pollock was convinced that America's economic future—and his own prosperity as well—depended on free access to the Mississippi River. Governor Gálvez, for his part, believed strongly that British bases near Louisiana—in places like Natchez and Mobile and Pensacola—presented a constant threat to Spanish interests in the region.

When war broke out between the Americans and British, American officers disguised as backwoodsmen canoed into New Orleans and, under the watchful eye of Pollock and protected by Spanish guards, loaded canoes with kegs of Spanish gunpowder. The officers then rowed their cargo back to Fort Pitt—the site of Pittsburgh—where it then made its way to Virginia. Governor Gálvez also helped the Americans by protecting their shipping vessels from the British so that goods such as furs, tobacco, flour, and lumber could be exchanged for badly needed guns, hardware, and medicine from Europe.

All the while Governor Gálvez was helping the American effort, he was also hoping that Spain, too, would soon declare war on Britain. Gálvez badly wanted England to be forced to return territory on the American continent—western Florida and the eastern side of the Mississippi as far north as the mouth of the Ohio River—that rightfully belonged to Spain. He felt all he needed to do was wait until troops from British forts there were called to the battlefields of Virginia and Pennsylvania. Then he would attack the forts with British forces.

Finally, in May 1779, Gálvez received word from Madrid to proceed at once with the conquest of West Florida. By early September, Governor Gálvez was ready and led a small flotilla of sloops, keelboats, and pirogues upriver from New Orleans about 150 miles to Manchac. In a few hours, Britain's Fort Bute fell. A week later, with a combined force of Spaniards and Indians, carrying every weapon from guns to tomahawks, they took Baton Rouge. In the terms of the surrender, the British gave up Natchez and the land beyond the Yazoo River Boundary of West Florida. With their boats full of prisoners and captured goods, Gálvez ordered his army back to New Orleans.

Later that fall, however, Gálvez and his flotilla left New Orleans again, heading for Britain's Fort Charlotte at Mobile. This time warships carrying Spanish marines were brought in from Havana, Cuba. They took the fort on March 15, 1780.

Now the only British base in the Gulf of Mexico was at Pensacola. It was well-manned, with nearly 1,000 soldiers stationed there. Gálvez planned for a year to put together an army strong enough to take it. By the spring of 1781, he had assembled 7,000 men, including troops from the Gulf and the Caribbean. The stunned British surrendered Pensacola after several days of fierce fighting.

Governor Gálvez's brilliant strategy helped Spain reach her peak of power in the Americas. The Spanish now controlled both banks of the Mississippi and eastern Louisiana as far north as the Ohio River. They held 5,000 miles of shoreline around the Gulf of Mexico —from Havana to Florida to the Mississippi Delta all the way to the Yucatán Peninsula of Mexico. What's more, Spain also owned the vast unknown from Texas and St. Louis over the Rockies to the Golden Gate and San Francisco Bay.

For his part in capturing such an empire, Bernardo de Gálvez was made viceroy of Mexico, where he served until his death in 1786. Later, Texas's beautiful bay of Galveston was named for this bold and intelligent leader.

Bay of Galveston

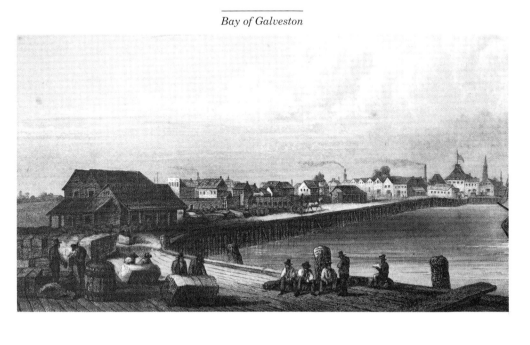

Part Three

America from Sea to Sea

By the early nineteenth century, Mexico was ready to cut its ties with Spain. Any feelings of loyalty to the mother country had long since been replaced by bitterness over a weak, selfish colonial government. What's more, there were scarcely any "pure" Europeans left in Mexico. Instead, many Mexicans could point, for example, to a Mayan grandmother, a Yaqui grandfather, and other relatives who'd spent so many years in the Americas that their Spanish bloodlines were hard to trace. As one observer noted, "There are no old Spanish families. . . . Old Spanish families are an invention of the gringo."

By 1821, Mexico had achieved its independence. As army officers struggled for power in Mexico City, however, the provinces far to the north were largely neglected. The California rancheros thrived as Mexico looked the other way—thrived, that is, until the Americans began arriving from the east. In Arizona and New Mexico, many local leaders such as Father Antonio José Martínez of Taos, held tight reins over their small parishes. When their power was threatened by the likes of Kit Carson and Stephen Kearny, they fought hard—and successfully—to hold on. In Santa Fe, where soldiers and traders of many countries met, María Barceló ("La Tules") found it to her advantage to switch loyalties from Mexico to the United States.

By the end of the nineteenth century, America's need to stretch out across the continent had created its present borders. Many Mexicans, like Estevan Ochoa and Mariano Vallejo, made the best of their new nationality. Others, such as Francisco Ramírez and Tibirico Vásquez, accused Anglos of stealing Mexican lands.

In 1898, the United States fought Spain after difficulties in Cuba. By the end of the Spanish-American War, though, America itself controlled both Cuba and Puerto Rico. In only a few years, huge numbers of immigrants from those islands would begin arriving in Miami and New York City. The United States, which in 1800 seemed small and innocent, was about to take on all the responsibilities— and problems—of a major world power.

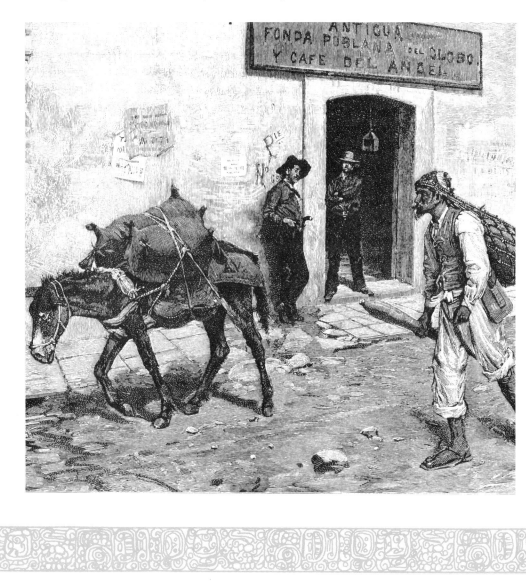

Manuel Lisa

Trader, Explorer

1772–1820

When eighteen-year-old Manuel Lisa arrived in St. Louis from New Orleans in 1790, he had wanted nothing but the world. If I set up trading posts and forts on the upper part of the Mississippi, he thought, I can build my own empire and control the destiny of half the American continent. He was so eager for money and power that he was willing to work twice as hard as anyone else. "I will go a great distance," he once explained, "while some are still considering whether to start today or tomorrow."

Lisa cared little about making friends, and, in fact, during his long career, he had very few. The explorer Meriwether Lewis hated him. James Wilkinson, Governor of Upper Louisiana, feared him. French traders on the Mississippi didn't hide their wish to see him dead—by their own hands if need be. Still, dislike for Lisa was mixed with admiration as his drive and imagination impressed even his enemies.

Lisa was clever and ambitious. When the Lewis and Clark expedition of 1803 opened up the northern part of the Missouri River, he grasped quickly the importance of the discovery. Governor Wilkinson would not allow Lisa to use St. Louis as a base for trade with the Spanish in Santa Fe, so instead he looked north. In 1807, he and forty-two men undertook an expedition up the Missouri.

Led by one of Lewis and Clark's guides, Lisa's expedition made its way up the winding river, past the great bend in North Dakota, and then down the Yellowstone River into central Montana. At this point, the men stopped and built a makeshift fort. From this fort, called Manuel's Fort, exploring parties headed off in all directions, and, in effect, opened up the country around the upper part of the Missouri River. Lisa became a trading partner with nearly all the Indian tribes in the region.

As men from Lisa's company went farther into the wilderness, rumors were started among other traders that Lisa was looking for a "back door" to Santa Fe and that his real goal was, in fact, to establish illegal trade with the Spanish. One of Lisa's explorers had spread the word that Indians around Montana's Big Horn Basin knew of Spanish outposts just a few days to the south. What's more, near these outposts was a great river that led directly to Santa Fe. If Manuel Lisa could find that river, he could get to New Mexico's trading center before anyone found out.

Many exploring parties left Manuel's Fort, but finding the Spanish settlements was much more difficult than anyone had imagined. One of Lisa's men, John Colter, traveled alone across the snow-covered peaks of the Big Horn and the Grand Tetons in the winter of 1807. He was the first white man to look down upon the lovely sight of Jackson Hole. Another, George Drouillard, drew a rough but accurate map of the region. The map contained just one error. Like all other explorers of the time, Drouillard thought Santa Fe was just south of what today is Montana and Wyoming. It wasn't until another exploring party from Manuel's Fort actually tried to get to Santa Fe that Americans realized the central Rockies, including the entire state of Colorado, lay in between.

The success of Manuel's Fort brought both the Upper Missouri region and St. Louis to life. Manuel Lisa had shown other traders that, though dangerous, it was possible to do business with Indian tribes, and the rewards were enormous. Competition for goods soon became fierce. St. Louis, just a frontier settlement at the turn of the nineteenth century, now became a transportation, government, and banking hub. And, at the center of St. Louis's boom, was Manuel Lisa.

In fact, during the early nineteenth century, Manuel Lisa was the most influential person on the Western frontier. His explorers gave him information about geography and Indian tribes, which he then passed on to government officials. His advice was crucial to United States policy.

Fur trappers along the Missouri River

In 1809, Lisa along with several other prominent traders, including William Clark, who'd accompanied Meriwether Lewis up the Missouri, formed the Missouri Fur Company. Despite an auspicious beginning, the company soon ran into trouble. The venture suffered from fires, Indian hostilities, and a suspicious, overly watchful U.S. government. Also, there was increasing competition from another trading company, John Jacob Astor's Pacific Fur Company.

Still, Manuel Lisa continued to prosper in the Upper Missouri country. He became an Indian agent for the U.S. government and is credited with turning the Sioux Indians from bitter enemies to valued allies. He established Fort Lisa, north of Omaha, Nebraska, as the base of the Missouri Fur Company. As one of that state's first pioneers, Manuel Lisa became known as the "founder of Old Nebraska."

Manuel Lisa died in St. Louis in 1820 at the age of forty-eight.

Jackson Hole, Wyoming

The First Angelenos

Los Angeles's First Settlers

1781

In 1779, the Mexican governor of California, Felipe de Neve, began to worry that the Franciscan missions were becoming too rich and powerful. He came up with a plan for establishing towns, or pueblos, to blunt the power of the Franciscan friars and their leader, Father Junípero Serra. According to his Reglamento, each new pueblo would be given land, and any family willing to settle would be given a house lot, two fields, and several tools.

After finding a suitable site for a northern pueblo at San José in 1777, the Mexican authorities set about looking for land in the south. They found a site nine miles east of Father Junípero Serra's Mission San Gabriel, and they named the new pueblo for a nearby river, Neustra Señora la Reina de los Angeles del Río de Porciúncula. The Mexicans referred to it as simply El Pueblo. When the Americans arrived many years later, they found it easier to call it Los Angeles.

But Governor de Neve had a problem with his pueblo on the Río del Porciúncula: No one wanted to move there. He'd specified that at least twenty-four farmers and their families should settle the new pueblo. Neve realized quickly though that few in Mexico wanted to jump at the opportunity of moving to this far-off, unknown place. In the end, twelve men and thirty-four women and children from Sinaloa, Mexico, were recruited. This mixed group of Spanish, black, and Indian *paisanos*, or peasants, were the poorest of the poor. Life was so bleak for them in Mexico that any change in life-style was welcome.

The settlers were sent across the Gulf of California from Mexico to Baja California and then traveled north by horse and mule. It was a dusty, hot trip, and several became ill. One man died of smallpox, causing the whole group to be quarantined at the Mission San Gabriel for nearly three weeks.

Finally, near the end of August 1781, the settlers left San Gabriel and began the last leg of their journey to the banks of the river. They crossed a dry, sandy wasteland dotted with flat cacti and chaparral. When they arrived at the site, these new *pobladores*, or pueblo dwellers, gathered under a huge sycamore tree and prepared to camp. Governor de Neve noted the date as September 4, 1781. Today, this date is celebrated as Los Angeles's official birthday.

By November, the pobladores had built huts with earth roofs for protection from the winter rains. They were each given two fields for planting corn and three tools—a plow, a hoe, and an ax—to work their crops. Some also received a few horses, mules, and chickens. During their first planting season, they built a dam in the river to divert the water they needed for irrigation.

Despite the pueblo's promising start, Father Serra and the other friars worried about stealing and gambling and plain laziness among the settlers. In 1782, three families were deemed "useless to the pueblo and to themselves" by the Franciscans and run out of town by the Mexican authorities. (Where did they go? No one knows. There was nothing but wilderness for hundreds of miles.)

Despite such difficulties with authorities, by the mid-1780s El Pueblo was a prosperous Mexican town. There was a new chapel, and the mud huts had been replaced by proper adobe houses. There were enough cattle now that they grazed well beyond the borders of the town.

By 1786, the pobladores were officially given titles to their lands. Each of the first Angelenos scratched a cross on the official documents because none of them could read or write. Then each of the original families was rewarded for its bravery and hard work with a brand for the cattle.

The first Angelenos, whose lives just a few years before could hardly have been more humble, had become California's nobility. From the very start, El Pueblo de los Angeles was a land of opportunity—a place where, through some mixture of work and luck, dreams could come true.

Early Los Angelenos

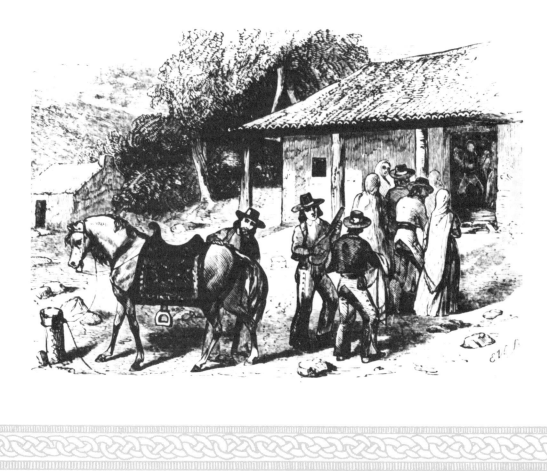

Father Antonio José Martínez

Priest, Educator

1793–1867

In the early 1830s, just after the territory of New Mexico passed from Spanish to Mexican control, the new government decided to raise money for public schools through fees on bars, saloons, and dance halls. The only problem with this scheme was that the so-called "sin tax" was entirely voluntary—in other words, customers only needed to pay it when and if they wanted to. By 1836, when almost no tax money had been collected and New Mexico's schools were in ruins, Father José Antonio Martínez decided to step in to help.

Padre Martínez, as he was generally known, was a native New Mexican, born in Abiquiu in 1793. He'd come to Taos in 1820 and soon became one of the town's most popular citizens. He was a Catholic priest, a scholar, and devoted to the welfare of his parish.

Education in Taos was in a hopeless mess. Almost no one, neither the Spanish nor the Indians, could read or write. What's more, after so many years of neglect, there were no teachers, no textbooks; there wasn't even a real classroom.

Padre Martínez opened his own school in Taos in 1835, teaching all subjects himself. He bought his own printing press—the first one in Taos—and issued textbooks, pamphlets, even a Bible. He became involved in political matters, too, including—as rumor had it—the Taos Uprising of 1847, during which the U.S. territorial governor was killed as villagers drove the Yankee intruders away.

He was well-loved in Taos, and it seemed he would live out his life there peacefully. Until, that is, one day in 1851 when the new church leader in New Mexico, Archbishop Jean-Baptiste Lamy, arrived for a visit.

Bishop Lamy was sent to New Mexico by Roman Catholic officials in Rome. Lamy was a Frenchman, who was already toughened by many years spent in the upper Great Lakes. He was devout, disciplined, and wanted to bring these same qualities to the small parishes of New Mexico. He ran into trouble almost immediately. Padre Martínez, who was nearly sixty by the time Bishop Lamy arrived to "change things," resisted the intrusion.

The American author Willa Cather wrote about the life of Bishop Lamy in her novel *Death Comes for the Archbishop*. In one chapter called "Padre Martínez," she describes the conflict between these two strong men. As Willa Cather describes him, Padre Martínez was a kind of parish dictator, who loved to flaunt his power. "The priest of Taos was not a man one would easily forget," she wrote. "One could not have passed him on the street without feeling his great physical force . . . he gave the impression of being an enormous man."

The bishop from France, however, was not impressed. He knew that "the day of lawless personal power was almost over, even on the frontier, and this figure was to him already like something . . . left over from the past."

By the time Bishop Lamy's visit in Taos was over, he'd grown to dislike Padre Martínez greatly. Even though the bishop knew that the padre was loved by his parishioners, Lamy felt the people of Taos would be better off without the old man's heavy hand on all town business. Finally, after a year in New Mexico, the bishop was so bothered by this parish priest of "disturbing, mysterious magnetic power" that he had him excommunicated.

Padre Martínez formed his own church and remained active in Taos. Much to the dismay of Bishop Lamy, Martínez continued to perform marriages and baptisms and last rites. But his power was lessening, both because he had abused it and because by 1860, New Mexico was not the backward territory it had been thirty years before.

Now New Mexico was American. And, according to Willa Cather, Padre Martínez "hated the Americans. The American occupation meant the end of men like himself. He was a man of the old order, a son of Abiquiu, and his day was over."

Padre Martínez died in Taos in 1867 and was buried in the churchyard. For better or worse, New Mexico would never see anyone quite like him again.

Pueblo of Taos

David Glasgow Farragut

American Admiral,
Civil War Hero
1801–1870

Two days before Christmas in 1861, Commander D. G. Farragut was called to Washington, D.C., by Gideon Welles, secretary of the Navy. Since the start of the Civil War in 1860, Farragut had been living in New York, far from his long-time home of Norfolk, Virginia. He was restless and worried: worried about the conflict, worried about his friends and relatives in the South, and worried that, at age fifty-nine, he was too old to play any part in the Union war effort. What, he wondered, could Secretary Welles possibly want with me?

David Farragut had been in the U.S. Navy since 1810, when he entered as a midshipman at the astonishing age of nine. The life of a Navy man, it seemed, was in David's blood. His father, George Anthony Farragut, had been born on the Spanish island of Menorca, but as a young man had set sail from his native land to fight in the American Revolution.

By the war's end in 1783, George Farragut was a decorated U.S. Navy officer. He then retired to Tennessee, married, and began raising a family. On July 5, 1801, his second son, James Glasgow Farragut, was born near Knoxville.

In 1807, the Farraguts left Tennessee and moved to New Orleans, where Major Farragut had been assigned to a new post. In 1808,

Mrs. Farragut died of yellow fever, leaving a shattered husband and five children.

In 1809, Captain David Porter, an old friend of Major Farragut, tried to help the family by offering to care for one of the children. Eight-year-old James Glasgow jumped at the chance to live with Captain Porter, who was a dashing naval hero. Porter saw that the boy had a great deal of promise, and he asked the secretary of the Navy to make him a midshipman. The secretary agreed, and in December 1810 James Glasgow Farragut—who changed his name to David in honor of Captain Porter—joined the Navy. When the War of 1812 broke out, David Farragut went to the Pacific with David Porter on board the Frigate *Essex*. Despite serving well during and after the war, he remained a midshipman for fourteen years. As Farragut later said, he spent too many years on shore "awaiting orders."

For most of his years in the Navy, in fact, David Farragut saw almost no action. He performed his duties well but often took time off to care for his ailing wife, Susan, who died in 1840. He married again a few years later, and, during the 1850s, his family settled in the Navy town of Norfolk, Virginia, hoping to stay there a good long time.

Such hopes were soon dashed when on December 20, 1860, several Southern states seceded from the Union. Virginia did not immediately join the Confederacy, and many families in Norfolk, including the Farraguts, hoped it wouldn't.

In April 1861, however, Virginia, too, seceded. The Farraguts were in despair. They had many relatives and close friends in the South and hated to leave. But David, now Commander Farragut, would not join the Confederate Navy. He decided instead to move from Norfolk to Hastings-on-Hudson, New York.

Once resettled in the North, Commander Farragut waited for his orders. Finally he was called to Washington, where he was astounded to be asked to lead the Union's naval expedition against the city of New Orleans. His orders told him to "proceed up the Mississippi River and reduce the defenses which guard the approaches of New Orleans, when you will appear off that city and take possession of it under the guns of your squadron."

David Glasgow Farragut had been waiting for this moment all his life. Finally, he had a chance to put his courage, honor, and intelligence to the test—at a time when his country needed him most. He set about preparing for this dangerous, difficult mission with astonishing thoroughness. On February 2, 1862, Commander Farragut was ready and headed for New Orleans in his steam sloop *Hartford*.

Battle of Mobile Bay

The battle began on April 18, with the Union bombardment of Fort Jackson on the west side of the Mississippi River just south of New Orleans. The bombing lasted several days with both sides suffering heavy losses. Finally, Farragut made the bold decision to move his fleet upriver, past the Confederate forts that protected the Queen City.

At dawn on April 24, seventeen Union ships steamed past the forts. What followed, as Farragut later wrote, was like "all the earthquakes in the world and all the thunder and lightning . . . going off at once." The fighting was fierce but Farragut managed to push into New Orleans, which he then captured easily. The taking of New Orleans was a great Union victory, and the credit went to the courage and energy of David Farragut. President Abraham Lincoln promoted him to Rear Admiral, making him the highest-ranking officer in the Navy.

After capturing New Orleans, Farragut wished to move on to Mobile Bay, but his orders were instead to head north. He and his forces took Memphis, then continued down the Mississippi, seizing Vicksburg, Galveston, and Corpus Christi. By the end of 1862, the Union held the entire Gulf Coast except the Confederate defenses at Mobile Bay.

Admiral Farragut had to wait until January 1864 for his chance to strike at this last holdout. Mobile Bay was particularly dangerous because its entrance was rimmed with torpedoes. As Farragut's fleet proceeded past the Confederate forts on either side, the lead ship hit a torpedo and sunk. When the second ship hesitated and cried a warning, "Torpedoes ahead!" Farragut, just behind in the *Hartford*, replied with his famous "Damn the torpedoes!" and went on at full speed. The *Hartford* took the lead, stormed past the forts, and entered Mobile Bay, victorious once again.

After this second stunning defeat, Admiral Farragut left active service. When the war was over, he traveled widely and was given a hero's welcome wherever he went. Shortly before his death, he was able to visit his father's birthplace on the island of Menorca. Thousands of proud citizens gathered to greet this American naval hero—"El gran Almirante Farragut," as they called him.

David Glasgow Farragut died while visiting Portsmouth, New Hampshire, on August 14, 1870. Since his death many monuments and memorials have been erected in his honor. Perhaps the best tribute, however, came from another war hero, Admiral George Dewey, who served under Farragut during the Civil War and who in 1898 was victorious at the Battle of Manila Bay. He wrote, "Whenever I have been in a difficult situation, or in the midst of such a confusion of details that the simple and right thing to do seemed hazy, I have often asked myself, 'What would Farragut do?'"

Admiral Farragut in the shrouds of his ship, The Hartford

Mariano Guadalupe Vallejo

Ranchero, Military Leader
1808–1890

When the American soldiers and settlers started to appear in California in the early 1830s, Mariano Vallejo thought the best thing to do was make friends with them. There was no point, Señor Vallejo told the other California rancheros, in ignoring the Americans or telling them to go away—they will just keep coming back. He encouraged his fellow Californios to work with the Yankees, and, in 1846, during the Bear Flag Revolt, the Americans thanked Mariano Vallejo by throwing him in jail.

Vallejo was born in Monterey, California, on July 7, 1808. He began military service in the Mexican army in 1824 and was promoted rapidly. He supported such liberal ideas as breaking up the powerful Franciscan missions, which, until the 1830s, were still in tight control of nearly all of California. When the lands and livestock of the missions were finally given away, Mariano Vallejo took control of huge portions.

By the time Mariano married Francisca Carrillo of San Diego in 1831, he was already one of the wealthiest landowners in California. His ranch in Petaluma was stocked with more than a thousand head of cattle. At his other ranch in Sonoma, where he settled with his young family in 1835, the Vallejos entertained in a grand style, often inviting Americans to join the fiestas.

When Vallejo supported his friend, José Figueroa, in his bid to become Mexico's next governor of California in 1833, Figueroa rewarded Mariano by making him Commander General of California's northern region. General Vallejo then established a garrison at Sonoma and ably organized the defense of the California frontier from Indian attack. When Governor Figueroa died in 1835, Mariano Vallejo supported his own nephew, Juan Batista Alvarado, for governor and not the man chosen by the Mexicans. The result of the conflict was an uprising—one cannonball was fired at the Mexican governor's residence in Monterey—which led to California's being named a free state by the Mexican government in 1836. In 1838, Governor Alvarado made Mariano Vallejo commander of all California's military forces.

By the mid-1840s, however, General Vallejo and Governor Alvarado were no longer on speaking terms. Vallejo retired to Sonoma and ruled pretty much as he wanted. Against the wishes of Governor Alvarado, he encouraged American families to move into northern California, claiming he couldn't stop them even if he'd wanted to.

Then, on the morning of June 6, 1846, American riflemen roused General Vallejo from his bed. They'd come to proclaim a new Yankee republic and to take the general himself as their first hostage. During what became known as the Bear Flag Revolt, Mariano Vallejo and his brother, Salvador, were taken to Fort Sutter and kept in prison for two months. Their American guards humiliated them and stole their belongings. During their imprisonment, Salvador repeatedly scolded Mariano for giving the Americans land and money, and he made his brother promise not to be so generous in the future.

Any such promise, however, was beside the point because the Bear Flag Revolt was soon followed by a full-fledged takeover of California by American troops. The Californios fought bravely in both the north and south, but they were unprepared and overwhelmed by the U.S. forces. The Vallejos never forgave the Americans for the Bear Flag Revolt and the months of imprisonment. By 1848, however, with Mexico officially out of California, they tried again to achieve some kind of harmony.

Mariano Vallejo remained one of the Californio's strongest leaders. Just after California became a state in 1850, Vallejo was elected to the state senate and served one term. After retirement, he remained a strong presence in state politics. He lobbied long and hard to have his home district of Sonoma made the state capital, but in this, too, he was to be disappointed by the Americans.

Señor Vallejo spent the rest of his life at his ranch, where he devoted himself to his large family and to the new winemaking industry that he'd helped establish in Sonoma and neighboring Napa Valley. Just before his death in 1890, Mariano Vallejo looked back over his long, productive life and said, "I had my day. It was a proud one."

Vicente Martínez Ybor

Cigar Manufacturer,
Founder of Ybor City

1818–1896

In 1886, France gave the United States a wonderful 100th birthday present: the Statue of Liberty. As though on cue, new immigrants from Spain, Italy, and many Eastern European countries began to stream past Lady Liberty. Vicente Martínez Ybor, who'd immigrated first from Spain to Cuba and then from Cuba to Key West, Florida, decided these immigrants—so eager to start new lives—were just the workers he needed for the industrial city he wanted to build near Tampa.

The idea for Ybor City had come when two Spanish friends of Martínez Ybor came to Florida to search for the mango and guava groves they thought grew wild there. (Guava paste was very popular in Spain, and a new source would be very profitable.) The two men didn't find any wild groves but they did find an ideal site near Tampa for a cigar factory, and they thought immediately of their friend. Martínez Ybor, they knew, had become dissatisfied with manufacturing cigars on the island of Key West. When they told Ybor, he went immediately to see the site for himself.

After visiting Tampa, Martínez Ybor agreed it was just what he was looking for. Tampa enjoyed a perfect climate and good supply of fresh water. And, unlike Key West at the time, it was easily reached by both land and sea. Within a year, Martínez Ybor had purchased forty acres of prime land and had begun to build not just a company but a company town.

Tampa was still recovering from the economic turmoil brought on by the Civil War. City officials were eager for Martínez Ybor to bring his cigar company to the area. So eager, in fact, that they gave him what he wanted most, complete control of both planning and building the new city.

Martinéz Ybor brought in his close friend, Gavino Gutiérrez, who'd earlier searched in vain for the mango grove, to design the factory. Mr. Gutiérrez borrowed from many different architectural styles. He designed brick factories with courtyards like the ones in Cuba; he gave the buildings iron balconies and railings popular in his native Spain; and he added the sparse workers' cottages, common in the Old South. In the spring of 1896, the *Tampa Guardian* wrote about the main factory building: "There is no more substantial structure in the State of Florida. None but the very best material had been used in any part and no expense spared to make it both handsome and convenient."

Martínez Ybor offered workers from Cuba, Spain, and other parts of Florida inexpensive housing; to investors and other manufacturers he offered free land and well-built factory buildings. By the end of 1886, the factories of Ybor City had already produced 1 million cigars. By 1900, that figure was up to 20 million, and, by 1919, many years after Martínez Ybor's death, 410 million cigars were produced in "Cigar City."

Despite Ybor City's prosperity, as the nineteenth century ended, labor unrest and political problems were on the rise. At this time, most of the workers were either Cuban or Spanish, and the revolution that was underway in Cuba in the 1890s made for very bad feelings between the two people. Political groups—some peaceful, some not—

sprang up within Ybor City. Strikes and demonstrations became common. Money that could have been spent building up the community was instead filtered to one side or another in the Cuban conflict.

Vicente Martínez Ybor died in 1896. There was a funeral cortege through Ybor City, and many workers marched, although not as one group. The mourners were instead divided up into their various ethnic and political factions unable to leave behind their differences even for one day.

Ybor City continued to grow, but it never became a unified town as Martínez Ybor might have hoped. The Spanish and the Cubans and, eventually immigrants from Italy, all lived separately, holding on to their own national identities for as long as they could. It would be several generations before Ybor City, which eventually became part of Tampa, could be considered a true community and not just a workers' settlement.

The California Rancheros

1830s

In the 1770s, when Gaspar de Portola and Father Junípero Serra blazed trails up and down the California coast, Spain's control of this distant province was firm. By 1821, however, Spain was ready to hand over her colonial outposts in the American West to Mexico. The Mexicans intended to govern California very differently from the Spanish, and they started by breaking up the all-powerful chain of Franciscan missions. The Mexicans took huge tracts of land from the church and parceled them out to native-born Hispanic families. These Californios, as they were called, suddenly rich in land and in livestock, settled into the easy life of the ranchero.

The word *rancho* was used to describe a farm devoted to cattle raising, although sometimes crops were planted there, too. (Mexicans refer to farms that raise only crops as haciendas.) In the 1820s and 1830s, California cattle ranches grew in both size and wealth, and the few families that owned the land became rich and powerful. The names are still familiar in California today: the Pachecos owned two ranches of 125,000 acres with 14,000 head of cattle, 15,000 sheep, and 500 horses. The Carillos and the Picos owned great ranches in the southern part of the province, and Mariano Guadalupe Vallejo, one of the most famous of the Californios, owned nearly unlimited land, including what are today the cities of Oakland, Alameda, and Berkeley.

The boundaries of these ranches were mostly a matter of guesswork. No one used surveying instruments; instead lengths of a lasso might be laid out from the back of a horse. Markers might be a pile of stones, a cactus bush, or a notched tree trunk. Because the lands held by each ranch were so vast, minor uncertainties in property lines didn't seem important, at least at the time.

Cattle were raised mainly for their hides. After drying in the hot California sun, the leather hides were taken by British and American ships to ports around the world where they were turned into saddles, harnesses, shoes, and other common items. The hides and tallow were in such demand that ranching families became very comfortable on the money and goods paid them by shipping merchants.

Life was sweet for the California rancheros. Money was plentiful, cheap labor was abundant, and almost no government taxes or regulation on ranching existed. Plus, the climate of coastal California was close to perfect. There seemed little reason to work hard or worry, and the Californios did neither. The shipping merchants who visited the huge ranches scoffed at the rancheros' easy lives. "A community of loungers," one Englishman said of Monterey. Others referred to the rancheros as the mañanas—those who always found it easier to put something off until tomorrow.

The rancheros, however, did work hard at having a good time. One family or another was always planning a party to mark some occasion—a wedding, a birthday, a saint's day—and these fiestas often lasted for three days. Any gathering, however, was an excuse for singing and for dancing the jota, the borrego, the fandango, the bamba.

The most important social event was the annual rodeo. Because the lands were vast, and there were no fences, the cattle had to be separated and branded once a year. After each rodeo, families gathered for days of fiesta, which would include dancing, displays of horsemanship, cockfighting, and even bull fighting.

Still, for all their fiestas and leisure time, there was something very sad about the rancheros. Perhaps it was because theirs was a doomed society, as fragile as the eggshells the women liked to fill with cologne or fine scraps of pretty silver and gold paper. For, as the large Californio families sat in the sun strumming guitars and singing, American pioneers, eager for work and for land, were heading westward.

Tules Gertrudes Barceló
Influential Citizen of Santa Fe
18?–1852

Santa Fe, in the province of New Mexico, was a lively place in the 1830s. Trade along the Santa Fe Trail from Independence, Missouri, to Santa Fe and later on to Los Angeles brought thousands of people into the city each year. Three cultures—Spanish, Indian, and the newly arrived Americans—mingled at Santa Fe's plaza, or town square.

The plaza was surrounded by adobe-brick hotels and restaurants, which seemed to attract nearly everyone, young and old, rich and poor, "from the governor to the ranchero—from the grandest señora to the kitchen cocinera. . . ." Every night there was a kind of dance called a fandango: "To judge from the quantity of tuned instruments that salute the ear almost every night," wrote one rather stuffy visitor from the East, "one would suppose that a perpetual carnival prevailed everywhere."

When the good people of Santa Fe weren't spending their evenings dancing, they were usually playing their favorite game, monte bank. Monte is a Mexican card game, where a player bets on his or her luck against a dealer. And, the most skilled monte bank dealer in Santa Fe was a noblewoman named Doña Tules Gertrudes Barceló. Her establishment was the most popular in Santa Fe during the 1830s and, after a time, she became one of the town's richest citizens.

La Tules, as she was known, came from a wealthy family in the provincial town of Tome. Forced into an unhappy marriage early in her life, she did what many Mexican women would never dare— she escaped, alone, to Santa Fe. But her boldness came at a high price, because no matter how much respect she won as a businesswoman and cultural leader, rumor and controversy followed her.

Still, her position at the center of Santa Fe society gave her such a close view of the events of two countries that she became a key adviser to both the Mexicans and Americans. When the United States and Mexico were at war in the 1840s, soldiers and officers alike came to La Tules's establishment to dance, gamble, and talk politics. Doña Tules, whose opinion was always valued, listened and commented, as "the cards fell from her fingers as steadily as though she were handling only a knitting needle."

The life of La Tules passed easily from fact to fiction. She became the main character of a novel published in 1948 called *The Wind Leaves No Shadow*, and she has been celebrated in paintings and poetry as well. As New Mexico grew and became first a territory of the United States in 1850 and then a state in 1912, the wit and charm and fiery red hair of La Tules became part of the romantic legend of Old Santa Fe.

Francisco Ramírez

Newspaper Editor, Publisher

1830–1890?

"Oh! Fatalidad!" shouted the editorial of *El Clamor Público* in August 1856. "California is lost to all Spanish Americans!" The writer, Francisco P. Ramírez, was a Californio whose family had lost everything—land, cattle, and dignity—when the Americans took control of California in the 1840s. Now, Francisco, only twenty years old, had became a champion of his people's cause.

Francisco Ramírez began his newspaper career as a typesetter for the Spanish page of the *L.A. Star*. Yet he despised the *Star*'s pro-American editorials and longed to write more balanced ones himself. Finally, in 1855, he quit his job and began publishing a one-page Spanish-language weekly, *El Clamor Público —The Public Outcry*. It was Los Angeles's first Spanish language newspaper.

Soon, all Angelenos—Spanish and Anglo—were curious about this new paper, and they read it with great interest. Ramírez not only commented on politics but also wrote articles of general interest about California and its future. A state with so many natural resources, he wrote, can't help but prosper. End hostilities between north and south, he urged, and all Californians will benefit.

Francisco Ramírez was also one of the first California editors to comment on the issue of slavery, which in the East was pushing the country toward war. He stood up, too, for all Latinos, urging readers to use the term "American," to apply only to all citizens of the Western Hemisphere, not just those of the United States.

El Clamor uncovered long-forgotten facts of history and used them to give Hispanic-American Californians pride in themselves again. Did people know, for example, that Mexicans had discovered gold in California long before 1849? Did they know the contributions Spanish-speaking people had made to American history? "This is our own, our native land," he wrote. "But like it or not, we are now under the American flag, and there is every probability that we shall remain so for all time to come." Ramírez encouraged Hispanic Americans to either educate their children in both English and Spanish or return to Mexico or Latin America.

El Clamor Público became a very successful newspaper. It attracted as much advertising as the *Star*, most of it from Anglo store owners hoping to attract Spanish-speaking customers. After only one year in business, *El Clamor* moved into larger quarters near the center of Los Angeles.

In 1859, Ramírez, confident of his popularity within the community, ran for the city assembly. He won only 25 percent of the vote in what was a terrible blow to his own confidence and, as it turned out, to his newspaper. After Ramírez's defeat, money problems plagued him. He tried to raise funds to stay in business, but failed, and on December 31, 1859, he published *El Clamor Publico*'s last issue.

Why did *El Clamor Público* fail? Francisco Ramírez's editorial voice had become too shrill for most of his readers. He attacked the U.S. government constantly, thereby driving away Anglo advertisers. By the end, he was out of step with all but his most liberal readers.

In many of his later editorials, Ramírez told readers that if they were fed up with California, they should return to Mexico. In 1860, he did just that. During the next few years, he held several positions in the Mexican government. In 1865, however, Francisco Ramírez returned to Los Angeles, serving for a time as the city's postmaster.

Later, Ramírez took over as editor of another Spanish-language newspaper, *La Crónica*, but he stayed there, too, only a short time. After 1872, nothing more was heard from this pioneering newspaper editor.

A view of early Los Angeles

Estevan Ochoa

Businessman, Civic Leader, Mayor of Tucson

1831–1888

Before Tucson, Arizona, had an airport or an interstate highway or even a railyard, Estevan Ochoa was the king of the city's transportation industry. Born in Chihuahua, Mexico, into a rich shipping family, young Estevan rode on his father's freight trains throughout northern Mexico, the southwestern United States, and even to the start of the Santa Fe Trail in Independence, Missouri. When it was time for him to begin his own career, there was no question what he would do—shipping was a part of him like the blood that flowed through his veins.

"Shipping," or freighting as it was also called, in the mid-1800s, meant the hauling of goods by wagon train. The first load of goods ever carried from Yuma to Tucson arrived in February 1856 on a fourteen-mule pack train. Several years later, when wagon trains replaced pack mules, several Mexican entrepreneurs invested in this new business. By the end of the Civil War in 1865, freighting was Arizona's most important business. Estevan Ochoa, along with his partner P. R. Tully, was at the helm of a vast shipping empire.

Tully and Ochoa was not only a huge freighting business but also a kind of department store, supplying both Tucson and the remotest forts and ranches with everything from harnesses and wagons to shoes. Later, the company became involved in mining and even sheep ranching. Estevan Ochoa became well-known for his keen business sense. "No other man," wrote the *Tucson Citizen* in 1874, "has given as much thought and attention to the development of the capacities of our country as Mr. Ochoa. He's always watching for something to introduce."

Estevan Ochoa and his wife, Doña Altagracia, brought grace and elegance to what had been a rough, frontier town. During the 1870s the Ochoa home was Tucson's finest and the couple entertained lavishly. Doña Altagracia dressed in silks and pearls and was followed about her mansion by a pet peacock, which fanned its plumes in front of startled guests and ate food from their hands.

The rise of Estevan Ochoa and of his firm, Tully and Ochoa, is partly the story of an ambitious and talented man and partly that of a community, Tucson, which welcomed Mexicans and allowed them to prosper. By 1860, most of California's native Hispanics had lost their great ranches and were struggling to earn a living. In Phoenix, Arizona, and in Texas, Anglo-Americans were in control and were not helpful either to the native Hispanics or to newcomers from Mexico.

But Mexicans were in control in Tucson and held the most important positions in town. They thrived in business, politics, the arts, and especially, education. The Mexicans of Tucson—called the Tucsonenses—founded many new schools during the 1870s, both public and private. Ochoa himself helped lead the fight to found the public school system of Arizona. As chairman of the committee on public education in 1871, he introduced a bill which, for the first time, allowed the state to levy property taxes to support the schools.

Estevan Ochoa's commitment to public education stemmed from his strong belief that Mexicans who wished to live and prosper in the United States needed a good education and an excellent knowledge of English. English language instruction, he once said, was as "indispensable as our daily bread." Only by learning English, he felt, could Mexicans compete with their American neighbors. He supported several public education bills that mandated English instruction in all Arizona schools.

The combination of loyalty and flexibility helped make Estevan Ochoa and other members of Tucson's Mexican community so successful. They were Catholic, spoke Spanish, and helped start private and parochial schools for their children. Yet they learned English, supported public education, and worked closely with white Americans when this was necessary.

Estevan Ochoa was so successful at bridging the two cultures that in 1875, he was elected mayor of Tucson. He and other Mexican-American leaders were respected both by their own people and by the city's Anglo community.

In November 1880, the railroad track into Tucson was completed and shortly afterward a great steam engine barreled into a Tully & Ochoa freight wagon, killing two mules. The shipping industry's future had arrived with a bang, and, unfortunately, Estevan Ochoa could only stand by and watch. He had not heeded the warnings of many that the railroads would take over from the mule pack, and when the Southern Pacific Railroad completed its route through Arizona in 1881, Ochoa and Tully began to fail. Before long, Ochoa was forced to sell much of his equipment at a loss just to keep his business alive.

Estevan Ochoa lived out his life in dignity. When he died in 1888, all members of Tucson society turned out to honor this respected man.

Rafael Chacón

Soldier, Memoirist

1833–1925

"I was born on the twenty-second day of April in the year 1833, at the ancient city of Santa Fe, in the Territory of New Mexico . . ."[8]

So begin the memoirs of Rafael Chacón, a man who saw firsthand the events that shaped New Mexico during the nineteenth century. When Rafael was in his seventies, his grandchildren urged him to write down all he had seen and done during his long life. His memoirs, they knew, would help all New Mexicans understand how their state changed from a remote Mexican province to a reluctant American territory and finally, in 1912, became the forty-seventh state.

In 1837, when Rafael was only four years old, his father held him in his arms to watch the Rebellion of La Cañada, during which the poor of the northern territory staged an uprising and murdered a hated Mexican governor. Almost ten years later, Rafael's father handed his teenage son a pair of pistols and told him to use them against the invading American forces. In another decade, however, Rafael Chacón was a loyal soldier of the United States, serving under Kit Carson in the battles against the Ute and Apache Indians.

Rafael Chacón had scarcely put down his guns to resume his life as a farmer and trader when he was forced once again to put on a military uniform. The year was 1860, and his uniform this time was Union blue. By 1861, New Mexico's military officials knew an invasion of New Mexico by the Confederate forces of Texas was close at hand. They also knew that the dreaded Tejanos were much better prepared for war than the New Mexicans. Captain Rafael Chacón was assigned to lead Company K of the First Infantry— an almost entirely Spanish-speaking regiment.

On the sixteenth of February 1862, the Confederate forces under the command of General Sibley were seen on the south side [of the Río Grande] near Fort Craig, a force of about three thousand armed men. At one o'clock in the afternoon they made a demonstration, forming a battle line on the southeast side of the fort for the purpose of sounding out our force or examining our positions. Our army also formed in order to fight outside the fort. . . . We shot perhaps three cartridges per man, and they killed a sergeant from Deus's company and wounded another soldier. Those were the first shots of the Civil War in our territory. . . .

About one o'clock in the afternoon, a single piece of Texan artillery appeared at the foot of the mesa, and with it they began a constant barrage that seemed deliberately directed only at the spot where my company was positioned. I observed that I had no support from our artillery to silence this piece, and in order to put it out of commission I had to make a charge on that position. Upon seeing our advance, the enemy artillerymen fled, leaving the gun in their flight, and one of my soldiers . . . with three or four others, went forward and seized it, lassoing and hauling it, cowboy fashion, to our lines where we had it all day until the afternoon, when, by superior orders, we were compelled to abandon the battlefield.

At the hour the sun went down the order was given to retreat. I, who already found myself very deep into the enemy zone because of the violence of our attack, did not understand the order at first for we considered that our charge upon the enemy's main cavalry had won the battle. I was so loath to leave the field that my company was the last of our army to retreat and cross the river. . . . The regiment of Colonel Carson fought bravely . . . they would have retaken the guns that the enemy had captured if the retreat had not sounded just as they were advancing on the enemy for that purpose. . . .[9]

The Battle of Valverde was the Westernmost battle fought during this gigantic conflict. It was also one of the bloodiest of the early part of the war, and, even though it appeared to be a defeat for the North, the Confederate troops of Texas were left so crippled by the battle that they never recovered their strength.

After the Union Army's defeat, General Sibley blamed the loss on what he said were the badly trained volunteers and militiamen of New Mexico. This official report was accepted for several years until finally, well after the war's end, the battle was reviewed, and the loss was found to be caused by errors of judgment at the highest level. The native sons of New Mexico, it was revealed, fought bravely against tremendous odds.

After the Civil War, Chacón returned to family life only to be called again a few years later to fight the Navajos. These tragic battles resulted in the Indian tribes being removed from their homelands in Arizona.

Rafael Chacón spent the end of his life in a part of northern New Mexico that in the late 1800s was added to the territory of Colorado. Chacón and several other Hispanic families resettled in the village of Trinidad. Trinidad was a part of the legendary Old West, home at one time to Bat Masterson, Doc Holliday, and Wyatt Earp. It was here that Rafael Chacón, comfortably well-off and surrounded by a large family, began writing his memoirs. He died in Trinidad in 1925, at the age of ninety-two.

Loreta Janeta Velázquez

Confederate Soldier

1842– ?

Loreta Velázquez wanted to be a soldier even more than her husband. When he reluctantly joined the Confederate Army in 1861, she kissed him goodbye and waved as he marched off to war. Then, not being one to sit on the sidelines, she headed for New Orleans, found a tailor, "who understood how to mind his own business," and soon changed herself from Madame Velázquez to Lieutenant Harry Buford, CSA.

Loreta never worried about doing what others expected of her. Born of aristocratic Spanish parents in Havana, Cuba, in 1842, she was scarcely fourteen when she eloped with her future husband, a handsome officer in the U.S. Army. When the Civil War began, the couple was living at Fort Leavenworth, Kansas. To the despair of her husband's fellow officers, Loreta became a passionate supporter of the Confederacy. She even managed to convince her husband to leave his post as a career officer in the U.S. Army and fight instead for the Southern cause.

Once Loreta herself put on the grey uniform of the South, she organized a volunteer battalion, dashed off to Pensacola, Florida, and headed for her husband's post. He was, needless to say, astonished to see her. He confessed that he was proud of her "gumption" but pleaded with her to return to civilian life. But Loreta was "wild about war" and wouldn't think of leaving. Shortly afterward, Loreta's husband was killed accidentally while loading his own gun. With his death, she was left completely alone in the world—alone to do exactly as she pleased.

The rest of Loreta Velázquez's life is an odd mixture of fact and fantasy, which she described in her autobiography, called *The Woman in Battle*. She continued her disguise as a Confederate soldier for several more years. She served first as a temporary company commander under General Bee at the First Battle of Bull Run, also called Manassas, in 1861. She remembered the battle as a glorious experience:

> The morning was a beautiful one, and the scene presented to my eyes was one of marvelous beauty and grandeur. I cannot pretend to express in words what I felt as I found myself about to engage in a deadly and desperate struggle. The supreme moment of my life had arrived and all the aspirations of my romantic girlhood were on the point of realization. I was elated . . . fear was a word I did not know the meaning of.[10]

Loreta Velázquez/Lieutenant Buford fought again at the Battle of Shiloh in 1862. By 1863, however, her career in the army came to an end. On her way to join Tennessee's 21st Regiment, she was wounded in a minor battle and taken to a doctor who discovered her secret: "I never saw a more astonished man in my life . . . ," she wrote in her memoirs.

After appearing before a military court and spending a brief time in jail, Loreta resumed a "normal" life. For Loreta Velázquez, however, normal meant darting all over the country spying for the Confederacy. When the war was over, she continued traveling constantly, although this time to talk to enthralled audiences about her war experience. In later years, the truthfulness of some of her accounts was called into question. She did serve in the Confederate Army but her career as a spy is at best "mysterious." There is no doubt though that Loreta Velázquez had a taste for adventure—and adventure is what she found!

The Battle of Shiloh

The Treaty of Guadalupe Hidalgo

The peace treaty that ended the long war between the United States and Mexico was signed at the Mexico City suburb of Guadalupe Hidalgo on February 2, 1848. It was soon ratified by both countries and proclaimed on July 4.

The terms of the treaty gave the United States about half the area of the Mexican Republic, including California, Texas, and all the land in between. The United States was, in turn, obliged to pay Mexico $15 million and assume the claims of U.S. citizens against Mexico, which totaled about $3.25 million. Any Mexican citizen remaining in the new American territory could become a U.S. citizen with full constitutional rights.

The treaty, however, was never fully honored, especially Article VIII. This article guarantees all Mexicans, whether choosing to stay in the United States or not, rights to all their lands. Shortly after the treaty was proclaimed, Mexican-owned lands were seized by Americans for one of many reasons—and sometimes they were just stolen for no reason at all. U.S. ranchers, businessmen, and railroad tycoons were so eager for these valuable lands that they used any flimsy excuse to seize them. The U.S. Departments of the Interior and Agriculture also grabbed as much as they could from the Mexicans. Within 100 years, Mexicans and Mexican Americans lost 4 million acres of land to private owners and 15 million acres to U.S., state, and local officials.

Had the terms of Article VIII, printed below, been fully honored—or been clearer from the beginning—perhaps generations of Mexican bitterness and hatred toward Americans could have been avoided.

Treaty of Guadalupe Hidalgo
February 2, 1848

Article VIII

Mexicans now established in territories previously belonging to Mexico, and which remain for the future within the limits of the United States as defined by the present treaty, shall be free to continue where they now reside, or to remove at any time to the Mexican Republic, retaining the property which they possess in the said territories, and removing the proceeds wherever they please, without their being subjected on this account to any contribution, tax, or charge whatever. . . .

In the said territories, property of every kind now belonging to Mexicans. . . shall be inviolably respected. The present owners, the heirs of these, and all Mexicans who may hereafter acquire said property by contract, shall enjoy. . . guarantees equally ample as if the same belonged to citizens of the United States.

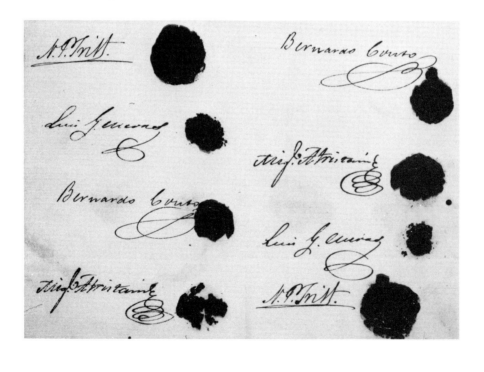

Tibirico Vásquez
The Great Bandido
c. 1845–1875

Tibirico Vásquez was a bit like Robin Hood, stealing from the rich and giving to the poor. In the 1870s, Vásquez ambushed stage coaches traveling west to San Diego or Los Angeles and robbed Anglo-American passengers of all their possessions. He then used the money to support his band of freedom fighters. The Anglos, Vásquez believed, took California away from its rightful owners, and it was now up to the native Californios to get back whatever they could.

California had been admitted as a state the Union in 1850. By the 1870s, the former El Pueblo de la Reina de los Angeles had become the bustling settlement of Los Angeles. There were many Anglos in southern California who'd become wealthy from a combination of trade, luck, and the seizing of lands from the native Californios—many of them former rancheros—through various tax schemes.

The native Californios were understandably bitter about losing control of their lands. Some moved to Mexico, others tried to work with the Anglos. Still others, like Tibirico Vásquez, decided to wage guerrilla war against the enemy.

In another era, Tibirico Vásquez might have lived comfortably as a *caballero*, a kind of gentleman cowboy. His family was descended from the first Mexican settlers of the pueblo that later became Los Angeles. When, by 1700, the small settlement began to prosper and grow, the first families acquired large tracts of ranch land, and some became very wealthy. By the 1840s, however, when California became first a territory and then a state, lands owned by Mexicans were gradually taken away. By the end of the nineteenth century, native Californians like Vásquez were left with nothing but their wits and wiles.

To many Californios, Tibirico Vásquez was a hero. To the authorities of the state of California, on the other hand, he was a criminal, pure and simple. By 1874, State Sheriff Billy Rowland had had enough of Vásquez's lawlessness and vowed to catch the slippery bandido any way he could.

Sheriff Rowland was helped by the U.S. government, which offered an $8,000 reward for Vásquez's capture. One of Vásquez's men couldn't pass up that much money and sent Rowland a message telling him of Vásquez's remote mountain hiding place.

At 1:30 A.M. on May 13, 1874, a seven-man posse sneaked onto the ranch where Vásquez's gang was hiding. The sheriff's men waited until noon of the next day before storming into the house. As they entered, they saw Vásquez heading out a back window. They yelled for him to stop. When he didn't, they opened fire, shooting the fugitive as he jumped onto his horse. Vásquez fell to the ground and told Rowland's men to hold their fire.

He was taken to the city jail in Los Angeles, where he became an instant celebrity. Lines of important visitors streamed into the jail to sit and chat with the famous bandido. Word spread that he was cheerful and charming and well-mannered. The doctor who attended his bullet wounds told reporters that he'd never seen a braver man.

The jury listened sympathetically as Vásquez told about leaving home at a young age: "I got mother's blessing and told her I was going out into the world to suffer and take my chances."

When the judge asked him to explain, Vásquez replied: "that I should live off the world and perhaps suffer at its hands."

Unfortunately for Vásquez the jury wasn't as charmed by his life story as the press and public. When the testimony ended, Vásquez was found guilty of robbery and murder. The judge sentenced him to death, and, on May 14, 1875, Tibirico Vásquez was hanged. With his death, the era of the Mexican bandido came to a close.

Juan Guiteras

Medical Researcher

1852–1925

For generations, yellow fever was known as the "pest of pests." A dangerous and deadly disease, it seemed to strike randomly throughout the world's tropical and subtropical regions. What caused the dreaded epidemics? Why, in some tropical villages, did many die while others were unaffected? During the late nineteenth century, medical researchers such as Juan Guiteras visited hospitals in Cuba and the West Indies, hoping to unravel yellow fever's terrible mystery.

Juan Guiteras had a special interest in Cuba's struggle with yellow fever. He was born on the island in 1852 and lived there until 1868, when for political reasons, his family resettled in the United States. Juan attended the University of Pennsylvania in Philadelphia and graduated from its medical school. He later taught at the university, specializing in tropical diseases, and practiced medicine at the University Hospital.

After years of research, Dr. Guiteras became the first to advance the theory that children living in areas where yellow fever was common could develop an immunity to the disease. This immunity came about after many mild bouts of yellow fever during childhood. These attacks would not be life-threatening; in fact, the children often were barely sick. This theory became very important in answering the question of how this disease was passed.

Dr. Guiteras came to agree with the theories of another Cuban researcher, Dr. Carlos Finlay, who suspected the culprit was an ordinary mosquito. Before Dr. Finlay's ground-breaking research, it was thought that yellow fever was caused by "something in the air." But if the cause were not some sort of living messenger, then why, Drs. Guiteras and Finlay wondered, were yellow fever epidemics common in Veracruz, Mexico, but not in Mexico City? The answer, they believed, was that Veracruz was located at sea level, where mosquitoes could breed. Mexico City, on the other hand, which lies 7,500 feet above sea level, was too high for mosquitoes, and consequently, for yellow fever.

Low areas in the land were common breeding places for mosquitoes, the cause of the spread of yellow fever.

It wasn't until the end of the nineteenth century that Dr. Finlay's theories were accepted more widely. The mosquito thought responsible for yellow fever was common in Havana, Cuba. When the Spanish-American War broke out in 1898 and large numbers of American troops arrived in the city, many were stricken by the disease.

Soon American and Cuban physicians began working together, visiting hospitals and diagnosing as many cases as they could. They noted all the peculiarities of individual cases, hoping to narrow the possible causes. Other diseases, such as typhoid and malaria, were also common in the Caribbean.

Finally, in 1901, a team of doctors lead by Walter Reed proved the theories of Drs. Finlay and Guiteras. The disease, they found, was caused by a virus transmitted by the bite of the female *Aëdes aegypti* mosquito. With this knowledge, future epidemics could be prevented by eliminating the breeding grounds of these mosquitoes. From this time on, the incidence of yellow fever declined and hundreds of thousands of lives were saved.

After years spent studying and working at the University of Pennsylvania, Dr. Guiteras returned to Cuba during the early 1900s and lived there until his death in 1925.

Remember the Maine!

The Spanish-American War and Its Aftermath

By the end of the nineteenth century, Spain's treatment of its long time colony, Cuba, had become an international scandal. The United States and other European countries were finally becoming aware of the terrible living conditions of most Cuban people, many of whom were in concentration camps. Several countries pleaded with Spain to change its ways but the Spanish government did nothing.

Revolutionary Cuban groups tried to overthrow Spain's harsh rule and failed. The Spanish continued to crack down on all Cubans, taking the island's revenues from the sugar plantations and using the money to arm themselves against Cuba's own people. Several American newspapers, notably the Hearst- and Pulitzer-owned dailies, began to devote a great deal of front-page space to the Spanish atrocities in Cuba. The articles were always one-sided, leading Americans to feel Spain needed to be removed from Cuba, at any cost. The American president, William F. McKinley, was unsure of what to do. Many in Congress were against military action, and the president, too, didn't seem to want any conflict. Then, a series of "accidents" forced him to change his mind.

The most famous occurred on February 15, 1898, when the battleship *Maine*, sent by the Navy to check on reports of rioting in Havana, blew up in Havana harbor. Two hundred and sixty men were killed on board. The cause of the explosion was never certain, although evidence leaned toward a true accident. William Randolph Hearst, however, seized on the incident and urged the United States to strike back. "Remember the Maine!" his newspaper headlines screamed, and the battle cry led the United States to war in April 1898.

The Spanish-American War was short but the results were far-reaching. The Spanish lost their holdings in Cuba, Puerto Rico, the Philippines, and Guam. The United States was left, if not in control of the colonial empire, then at least in a much more responsible position than before. The end of the war pushed the United States into the world arena—it was now a major international power.

Just what the American role in Cuba would be was determined at a Constitutional Convention in 1900–1901. The result was the Platt Amendment, which stated that the American military would leave the island as soon as a legitimate Cuban government was in place. From 1900 until the next Cuban revolution in the 1950s, Americans would have great control over Cuba's affairs. Many Cubans, tired of the hard life in their native country, moved to America, and this flow of immigrants would change both countries forever.

Part Four

The Twentieth Century

The start of the twentieth century found Cuba, Puerto Rico, and Mexico in turmoil. Spain's archaic rule of its Caribbean possessions was challenged successfully in 1898, and now the United States was trying to help clean up the messes caused by years of neglect and mismanagement. In Mexico, thirty years of rule by the dictator Porfirio Díaz had left the lower classes desperately poor and most of the country's resources in the hands of a few wealthy Mexicans and foreigners. Revolt was inevitable, and it came in 1910. The bloody Mexican Revolution, which lasted several years, made daily life unbearable for the average citizen.

As ruler after ruler in these three countries tried and failed to establish order, many of their citizens moved north, hoping to find stability and prosperity in the United States. Most were poorly educated city slum dwellers or rural farm workers. In the United States, they faced discrimination. But, for those determined enough, there was also something that they'd not known in their homelands— opportunity.

The twentieth century also found many Hispanics enjoying the benefits of being second- or third- or even fourth-generation Americans. Families such as the Fuertes and the Alvarezes, for example, made the most of America's offerings in education. And, as the century's midpoint passed and all Americans began looking hard at their attitudes toward ethnic and racial minorities, many more Hispanics were poised to make great contributions to this country's arts, letters, science, sports, education, and government.

George Santayana

Philosopher

1863–1952

"Those who cannot remember the past are condemned to repeat it."—George Santayana

The facts about George Santayana's life are simple enough. He was born in Madrid, Spain, on December 16, 1863, to Agustín Ruíz de Santayana and Josefina Borras. After spending his early years in Avila, Spain, he moved to Boston in 1872 and lived there with his mother and stepbrothers and stepsisters. He attended the Boston Latin School and then Harvard University, from which he graduated with highest honors in 1886. After studying for a time in Europe, the young scholar returned to Harvard where he taught from 1889 until 1912. By that year, his careful saving and a small inheritance from his mother made it possible for him to retire from his teaching position and return to Europe, where he lived the rest of his life. He died in Rome in 1952 at the age of eighty-nine.

Beyond the facts of George Santayana's life and career are what really mattered to him—his writing, his reading, his reflections on the meaning of life's experiences. He was both a philosopher and a poet. He looked to the past to help him explain the present and the future, and he urged others—as his famous quote illustrates—to react to current events only after deep reflection of lessons learned by previous generations. We must note the rhythms and patterns of the past, he wrote, and only then will we learn and understand.

His first philosophical essay was *The Sense of Beauty*, published in 1896. In 1900, came *Interpretations of Religion and Poetry*. Seven years later, when Santayana was forty-five, he published his greatest work—and the one that brought him international fame, *The Life of Reason*. He didn't publish again until the 1930s when he gave the world *The Realms of Being*.

As Santayana's writings show, there were two distinct sides of his character, formed by his connections with both America and Europe. He had, he said, a transatlantic mind: one pole being the ancient walled city of Avila, Spain, and the other the New World intellectual center at Harvard. His allegiance to these two very different places—and his sense of not quite belonging to either—made him feel alone in the world. He called himself the "eternal stranger and traveler" and suggested these two roles were perfect for a philosopher.

In his great autobiographical work, *Persons and Places*, he discusses the different parts of his life in chapters with names such as, "My Mother," "My Father," "Avila." In the following excerpt from "I Am Transported to America," Santayana describes how, even as a nine-year-old, he was able to note many differences between the American and the European way of thinking.

> The day of our arrival was very warm with, the damp suffocating heat of the New England summer; there was naturally some confusion in landing, and everything seemed odd and unaccountable. . . . No docks; only a wooden pier raised on slimy piles, with the stained sea-water running under it; and on it a vast wooden shed, like a barn, filled with merchandise and strewn with rubbish. America was not yet rich, it was only growing rich; people worked feverishly for quick returns, and let the future build for the future. . . .

But what did I see here? . . . just in front of me, what first caught and held my attention was something like a large baby-carriage suspended high in air on four enormous skeleton wheels: Robert [Santayana's stepbrother] called it a buggy. . . . The front wheels were almost as large as the back wheels. . . . [T]his littlest of carriages could make only a great sweep and was in danger of upsetting at every corner.

Here by chance my eye, at the first moment of my setting foot in the new world, was caught by symbols of Yankee ingenuity and Yankee haste which I couldn't in the least understand but which instinctively pleased and displeased me. I was fascinated by the play of those skeleton wheels, crossing one another like whirling fans in the air, and I was disgusted by such a dirty ramshackle pier for a great steamship line. I think now that the two things expressed the same mentality. That pier served its immediate purpose, for there we were landing safely at it . . . what did it matter if it was ugly and couldn't last long? . . . As for the buggy, its extreme lightness . . . made speed possible over sandy and ill-kept roads. The modest farmer could go about his errands in it, and the horsey man could race in it. . . . Never mind if in the end it turned out to be like some . . . ambitious species of insect, that develops an extraordinary organ securing an immediate advantage but leading into fatal dangers . . . . The taste for it marks the independence of a shrewd mind not burdened by any too unyielding tradition, except this tradition of experimental liberty, making money and losing it, making things to be thrown away, and being happy rather than ashamed of having always to begin afresh.[11]

Arthur Alfonso Schomburg

Collector, Bibliophile

1874–1938

Arthur Alfonso Schomburg's childhood in Puerto Rico is cloaked in mystery. The man who grew up to be called "the Sherlock Holmes of Negro history" left few clues about his own life. He seems to have wanted students to look at his work—the vast Schomburg Collection of Negro Literature and History—and not bother with the details of his life.

This much, however, is known: his mother, Mary Joseph, was a black laundress, who'd come to San Juan from St. Thomas, Virgin Islands. Arturo's father, Carlos Federico Schomburg, was a German-born merchant. Carlos was stern and distant; Arturo seems to have barely known him. Mary, on the other hand was, as Arturo recalled, "loving and pure." She was determined that her bright son should get some kind of education. Unfortunately, schooling in Puerto Rico—at the time still part of Spain's rickety empire—was very limited. There were no free schools, and Arturo's mother could not afford tuition.

Arturo did manage to attend one elementary school in San Juan, and there he learned something very important: to hate racism. Black people, one teacher had told the eager student, had "no history, no heroes, no great moments." The young boy was stunned. Is it possible, he wondered, that my mother's people have contributed nothing to history or culture? Surely if someone were to dig deeply enough he would find enough history to fill a treasure chest! Arturo decided then and there that he himself would read and study and find the history, heroes, and great moments of black history.

Despite Arturo's love for Puerto Rico and its people, he realized that to make his mark in life he would have to leave the island. Life there was desperate. As one observer noted, it was a place not of "with's" but "without's": "without schools, without books . . . without newspapers . . . without political representation, without municipal self-government. . . . [T]he energies of our people are absorbed in the production of sugar to sell to England and the United States."

In April 1891, Arturo Schomburg left Puerto Rico and moved to New York City. He worked several jobs—bellhop, porter, printer—while attending night classes at Manhattan Central High School. He worked for a while with the other Puerto Rican and Cuban *tabaqueros* (cigar makers), who were famous for their lively discussions of politics and literature.

Arturo hadn't been in the United States long before he became aware of the plight of American blacks. By the beginning of the twentieth century, he was working actively to change conditions for all blacks and Hispanics. He wrote articles urging freedom for the people of Puerto Rico and Cuba and equality for all races in the United States. Why, he wondered, are blacks in America treated like second-class citizens? The words of his school teacher kept coming back to him—no history, no heroes. . . .

While still in his early twenties, Arturo began his life's work. He read and studied and collected the materials of black history and culture and began to make them available to other black scholars. He was neither a trained academic nor a librarian so he needed to support himself and his family with a "normal" job at New York's

Banker's Trust Corporation. Almost all his spare time, though, was devoted to sleuthing—that is, uncovering the rich past of the black people in the Americas. His goal was to "set the record straight." He hoped that by uncovering the richness of the past, he could help solve one of the problems of the present: racial prejudice. Arturo began corresponding with many of the most famous men of the day, including W. E. B. DuBois, Booker T. Washington, Marcus Garvey, and James Weldon Johnson. His private collection of books and pamphlets and letters became so large that it threatened to take over his family's home in Brooklyn. Visitors streamed through the rooms to look at the rare books, which were piled to the ceiling.

Arthur A. Schomburg (standing, second from right) with his staff and guests at the unveiling of a bust of the actor Ira Aldridge.

By the 1920s, Arturo began receiving offers to buy the collection. Its contents were, after all, of great interest to scholars from all walks of life. Arturo's painstaking efforts over twenty years had yielded, just as he'd hoped, many treasures: he had important first editions of the eighteenth century poet, Phillis Wheatley; letters and memorabilia from Haiti's liberator, Toussaint L'Ouverture; book plates and prints from West Indian artists. The contents of his Brooklyn home were described as the "most useful of all collections of black history."

Finally, in 1926, the New York Public Library purchased the collection with a grant from the Carnegie Corporation. The library then moved the 2,932 volumes, 1,124 pamphlets, and many prints and original manuscripts into a new branch on West 135th Street in Harlem. The Arthur A. Schomburg Collection of Negro Literature and Art was first opened to the public in 1934. Arturo then became the collection's curator, a position he held until just before his death in 1938.

In 1987, nearly fifty years after Arturo's death, the vast collection was moved to its own building. The Schomburg Center for Research in Black Culture is a fitting tribute to a man who spent his whole life trying to give black people, as he said, "the background for our future."

Louis Agassíz Fuertes

Artist, Naturalist

1874–1927

As far back as anyone in his family could remember, Louis Fuertes had two loves: nature and drawing. He particularly loved to sketch the trees, birds, and animals he saw near his home in Ithaca, New York. As Louis's daughter, Mary Fuertes Boynton, wrote in her introduction to her father's collected letters: "He and his sister Kippy (Mary Katherine) had their zoo under the front porch, and were from early childhood collectors of all kinds of natural specimens, alive and dead." Louis's mother tried not to worry about the menagerie, except when "forced . . . by the presence of a live owl tied by the leg to the kitchen table, a dead chickadee kept too long in the little coat pocket, or a skunk. . . ."

One day, when Louis was nine, a family friend, who'd noticed Louis's interest in birds, took the boy to the public library to look at a copy of John Audubon's *Birds of America*. Louis was awed by this great volume and returned to the library again and again to sit before its stunning pictures. They were, Mary wrote, "his daily bread. . . . even as a child he understood that Audubon was inspired by the same love of the form and beauty of birds that he himself was feeling."

By fifteen, Louis's mind was made up: He would spend the rest of his life studying and drawing birds.

Louis Fuertes was born in Ithaca and spent almost all his life in that upstate New York university town. His father, Estevan Antonio Fuertes, descended from a prominent Spanish family, was a civil engineer. He taught at Ithaca's Cornell University for many years and eventually became the Dean of the Department of Civil Engineering. Louis's mother, Mary Stone Perry, could trace her roots to New York's early Dutch and English settlers.

In 1894, when Louis was a sophomore at Cornell University, he traveled with the college glee club to Washington, D.C. He took along many of his bird drawings on the off chance that a fellow club member might introduce Louis to his uncle, the famous ornithologist, Elliot Coues. The meeting did take place, and Dr. Coues was so impressed with Louis's work that he offered to show the drawings to colleagues at a meeting of the American Ornithologists Union. "You would have felt proud and pleased," Dr. Coues wrote Louis, "if you had been present to see how well they were received and how highly they were praised." At twenty-one, Louis Fuertes was on his way.

After college, Louis continued to study both drawing and ornithology. In spring 1898, he began in earnest to increase his knowledge of the birds of North America. He first traveled to Florida, and in 1899, went to Alaska with the famous Harriman Expedition. This scientific expedition was financed entirely by the railroad magnate Mr. Edward Harriman and included many famous naturalists and conservationists, including John Muir and John Burroughs.

He later traveled to Texas, New Mexico, and then between 1902 and 1913, visited the Bahamas, Saskatchewan, and the Canadian Rockies, the Yucatán Peninsula of Mexico and Colombia, South America. His energy and thoroughness became legendary.

Just as impressive, in fact, as his stunning paintings and sketches, were the images imprinted on his mind. He had a photographic memory and never lost even the tiniest detail of each bird he examined. Coworkers spoke with awe of his intense concentration while examining a bird. At these moments, he forgot everything around him—as if only the artist and his subject existed.

His paintings illustrated the leading bird books published between 1896 and 1927 and are witness to the skill and devotion he brought to his subject. A fraction of books he illustrated include: *Birds of New York*, *Birds of Eastern North America*, *Game Birds of California*, and *Herons of United States*. In 1923, he became a lecturer in ornithology at Cornell University.

Settled in Ithaca with his wife and two children, Louis balanced his roles as a teacher, artist, and father. Then, in 1927, he was killed at a rail-crossing accident in Ithaca. He was 53.

At a memorial service held at Cornell University shortly after Louis's death, several friends and colleagues spoke lovingly about this great man. Mary Fuertes Boynton liked the following remarks of longtime friend, Dr. Frank Chapman, the best:

If the birds of the world had met to select a human being who could best express to mankind the beauty and charm of their forms, their songs, their rhythmic flight, their manners for the heart's delight, they would unquestionably have chosen Louis Fuertes.[12]

Pablo Casals

Cellist, Composer, Conductor

1876–1973

"From my earliest days," Pablo Casals, once told a friend, "music was for me a natural element, an activity as normal as breathing." Indeed, Pablo's father, Carlos, taught his young son to play the piano, violin, and organ. When a traveling minstrel's makeshift cello caught Pablo's eye, Carlos Casals fashioned one himself, using a gourd as sounding board. So, after such fatherly encouragement, no one could understand why, when the eleven-year-old prodigy was invited to study the cello in Barcelona, Carlos was dead-set against it. What use is studying the cello, he asked. My son should learn something practical, like carpentry.

Fortunately, Pablo's mother, Pilar, held firm and took her son to the Municipal School of Music in Barcelona. There he gave his instructors fits as he rebelled against the traditional stiff-arm way of playing the cello. "I freed the arms," was often the way Pablo Casals described his important contribution to cello-playing.

Later, in Madrid, he studied chamber music and composition with a scholarship given him by Spain's Queen Christina. Royal support, however, was withdrawn after Pablo's mother quarreled with the queen's music adviser, who had demanded that the boy compose Spanish operas. Pilar Casals insisted that for her son, the cello must come first.

After leaving Madrid, Pablo's mother took Pablo first to Brussels, Belgium, then to Paris, where the two lived in near poverty while Pablo studied the cello. In 1899, the twenty-three-year-old Spaniard made his all-important debut in Paris, playing Johann Sebastian Bach's unaccompanied suites for cello so brilliantly that audiences were overwhelmed by their beauty. From then on, the young musician was in constant demand, playing in concert halls throughout the world.

In 1920, he founded the Pau Casals Orchestra in Barcelona. ("Pau" means *Pablo* in Catalán. Casals was fiercely proud of his roots in Catalonia, which is in Spain's northeastern region and includes the lovely city of Barcelona.) He led the orchestra himself and discovered the great joys of conducting. An orchestra, he said, is "the greatest of all instruments."

Pablo Casals felt very strongly that artists could not ignore the rest of humanity and must pay attention to politics. When, in 1936, General Francisco Franco overthrew Spain's legitimate government, the famous musician made clear his opposition to the fascist leader. During the three-year civil war that followed, Pablo helped the Republican anti-Franco effort by holding benefit concerts. When in 1939, General Franco's forces claimed victory, Pablo Casals left his beloved Spain and vowed never to return while Franco was in power.

The maestro's early years of exile were spent in Prades, a French village close to the Spanish border. When during World War II, the forces of Nazi Germany occupied France, Casals stayed in Prades despite invitations to move to the United States. When the war ended and the fascist forces of Hitler and Mussolini were defeated, Pablo Casals was hopeful the Allies would help Spain remove Franco from power, too.

When, in 1945, Casals realized that the Allied forces had, in his view, abandoned Spain, he was so bitter and disappointed that he declined all further invitations to play or conduct and lived quietly in Prades, seeing only a few friends and students. In 1950, with the gentle prodding of an American violinist, Pablo Casals organized the first of the Prades Festivals. These annual Bach concerts continue to this day.

Pablo Casals and his wife María

In 1956, Pablo Casals emerged from his exile and gave a concert in Mexico. He then visited Puerto Rico, the birthplace of his mother. The next year, Casals left Europe and resettled near the island's capital of San Juan, where he lived the rest of his life. In August 1957, Casals married María Montanez, a Puerto Rican cello student, who was sixty years younger than her new husband.

After moving to Puerto Rico, Pablo Casals traveled often to the U.S. mainland, giving recitals at, among many other places, the United Nations and the White House. In 1962, he performed for President John F. Kennedy and the two became close friends. After President Kennedy's assassination in 1963, Pablo was deeply upset—to the point of depression—for at least a year.

The last ten years of Pablo Casals's long, fruitful life were spent at his seaside home in Puerto Rico with his devoted wife, María, seeing that the maestro's time was evenly divided between work and relaxation. Pablo Casals died in 1973 at the age of ninety-six. General Francisco Franco died two years later, in 1975, and shortly after the generalissimo's death, Spain began moving toward democracy. After vowing in 1939 that he would never live in Spain as long as Franco was in power, Pablo Casals missed the chance to return to his homeland by only two years.

All who knew Pablo Casals or heard his music were profoundly affected by this great man. In 1954, the German writer, Thomas Mann, himself one of the greatest artists of the twentieth century, said, "For me as for thousands of others, his very existence is a source of joy."

Adelina Otero Warren

Writer, School Administrator

1881–1965

During the 1930s, Adelina Otero Warren was the Santa Fe County, New Mexico, superintendent of schools. She traveled throughout the northern part of the state visiting small, remote schools and getting to know the teachers and families of the schoolchildren. A gifted writer, Adelina loved New Mexico and its Spanish-American people who, as she wrote, "have found peace and contentment in the canyons and the mountain tops."

Adelina's own family, the Oteros, had lived in New Mexico for several generations. They were, in fact, one of the state's most prominent families. Adelina's father, Miguel A. Otero, served as New Mexico's territorial governor from 1897 to 1906. (New Mexico became a state in 1912.)

The following story is from an article called "My People," which Adelina Otero Warren wrote in 1931.

> Many persons believe New Mexico is a region of plains. But it is in the northern part, into the fertile valleys of the Rio Grande, back into the mountains and their canyons, that my work as county superintendent of schools takes me. Into Cundiyo, situated 8,000 feet high in the Sangre de Cristo range, reached by a difficult road down arroyos and up over mountains.
>
> . . . Here is a typical mountain community, entirely occupied by Spanish-Americans, a gentle industrious, and intelligent people. The

houses are flat-roofed, and are plastered with adobe of a warm, brown color which conforms to the earth around. Wherever possible, space has been cleared for gardens and little farms fed by a stream of crystal water. In the background are the high pines. It is the fall of the year. The crops have been gathered from the mountain canyons. The men and women work together. Corn is husked and separated; the blue for tortillas and atole, the white for flour. Both will be taken to the water mill at Nambe to be ground. The yellow pumpkins are placed on the roofs; the chili, redder than any sunset, is hung in strings from the *vigas* to dry, and later will be ground into *chili molido*. Apples are sliced and placed on boards in the sun.

Since the road was bad, the school nurse and I left my car at Nambe, the Indian village, and hired an Indian boy to drive us in his wagon to Cundiyo. . . . Darkness comes upon us suddenly in the high mountains, like a curtain lowered to cover our eyes from too much grandeur! But we were fortunate. A moon rose over the range, shedding its white light upon the countryside. . . .

Suddenly I heard a man singing. I looked back and noticed that he was following us on horseback. It was Teofilo, one of the school directors.

I asked him, "Teofilo, where are you going at this hour?"

"*Para* Santa Fe, Señora."

"To Santa Fe! It is thirty miles. You will not arrive there till late. Can I attend to your business for you?"

"*No, Señora. No tenga pena.*" ("Do not be worried.")

We drove on. Our Indian boy never saying a word; Teofilo just keeping us in sight. The moon, as it rose, gave us more and more light. At first the tall pines seemed like sentinels one is afraid to approach, but gradually they became more friendly and Teofilo began to sing:

> *Alli, en un bosque donde yo me hallo, solo se oye mi*
> *triste penar.* (In a forest where I find myself alone,
> I hear my sad thoughts.)

The melody of it, the pathos, *"Solo se oye me triste penar!"* The little Spanish community; the mountains; the moon; Teofilo's voice breaking the great silence. *La Hermosura de la noche!* We finally reached Nambe, and as I thanked and paid the Indian boy and got into my car, I noticed Teofilo was still following. He drew up to the car and addressed me.

"Are you all right, Doña Adelina?"

"Si, gracias."

"You will not have trouble with your car?"

"I think not."

"Well, then, *buenos noches, y Dio la cuide.* I shall return to Cundiyo. But, first would you be so kind as to mail this letter for me in Santa Fe?"

"But you are not going there yourself, then?"

Teofilo smiled, bowed, donned his hat, and rode off into the night. He had followed us for ten miles to see that we were not lost in the canyon! Yes, these are my people, my friends.[13]

The Sangre de Cristo mountain range

Bernardo Vega

Tabaquero, Activist, Memoirist

1885–1965

"Early in the morning of August 2, 1916, I took leave of Cayey. I got on the bus at the Plaza and sat down, squeezed in between passengers and suitcases. Of my traveling companions, I remember nothing. I don't think I opened my mouth the whole way. I just stared at the landscape, sunk in deep sorrow . . . but ready to face a new life." [14]

After reaching San Juan by bus, Bernardo Vega boarded the *Coamo*, a ship that became famous for the thousands it carried from the Caribbean island of Puerto Rico to a new home and new life in New York City.

Bernardo Vega was part of the earliest wave of immigrants to leave Puerto Rico for the United States. In 1910, New York City had a native-born Puerto Rican population of only 500; by 1920, there were 7,000 and by 1930, 45,000. Many of the first arrivals were professional and tradespeople, who were fleeing the island's lack of opportunity and miserable living conditions.

On the fourth day of the journey, the immigrants's destination was in sight. Bernardo Vega wrote: "We saw the lights of New York even before the morning mist rose. As the boat entered the harbor the sky was clear and clean. The excitement grew the closer we got to the docks. We recognized the Statue of Liberty in the distance. . . . In front of us rose the imposing sight of skyscrapers— the same skyline we had admired so often on postcards. Many of the passengers had only heard talk of New York, and stood with their mouths open, spellbound. . . ."

At Staten Island, Bernardo got off the ship with the other *tabaqueros*, or cigar workers. In Puerto Rico, *tabaqueros* were considered among the best educated and skilled of all workers, and, as the men headed deep into Manhattan Island, they were confident they'd soon find work.

Tabaqueros *still make cigars by hand.*

But, after a short visit to a tiny cigar factory on Manhattan's Lower East Side, Bernardo realized finding work wouldn't be as easy as he'd hoped. "This dump hardly provides for us!" Thus, as Bernardo wrote, "My dream of rolling cigars in the Leon brothers's little factory was shattered. My tribulations in the iron Tower of Babel had begun."

There were, indeed, many hard times for immigrant workers during the early twentieth century, and Bernardo Vega, like many other Puerto Ricans, struggled to earn a living. He had belonged to a workers' union in Puerto Rico and became an early labor organizer in New York, too. He had little formal education by today's standards, but he set about educating himself. He read widely and became a skilled writer. He worked in New York City until the 1950s, when both for sentimental and political reasons, he returned to Puerto Rico to live out his life.

He wrote about his experiences in the "iron Tower of Babel" in *Memoirs of Bernardo Vega, A Contribution to the History of the Puerto Rican Community in New York*. In one of the early chapters, called "The Customs and Traditions of the Tabaqueros and What It Was Like To Work in a Cigar Factory in New York City," Bernardo tells about working at the El Morito Cigar Factory on 86th Street. His fellow *tabaqueros* were not only Puerto Ricans but Cubans and Spaniards as well. In the following excerpt, Bernardo tells about the official "factory reader," who read while the others rolled cigars.

He would read to us for one hour in the morning and one in the afternoon. He dedicated the morning session to current news and events of the day, which he received from the latest wireless information bulletins. The afternoon sessions were devoted to more substantial readings of a political and literary nature. A Committee on Reading suggested the books to be read, and their recommendations were voted on by all the workers in the shop. The readings alternated between works of philosophical, political, or scientific interest, and novels . . . chosen from the writings of Zola, Dumas, Victor Hugo . . . Tolstoy. All these authors were well known to the cigarworkers at the time.

During the readings at "El Morito" and other factories, silence reigned supreme. It was almost like being in church. Whenever we got excited about a certain passage, we showed our appreciation by tapping our tobacco cutters on the work tables. . . .

At the end of each session there would be a discussion of what had been read. Conversation went from one table to another without our interrupting our work. Though nobody was formally leading the discussion, everyone took turns speaking. When some controversy remained unresolved and each side would stick to a point of view, one of the more educated workers would act as arbiter. And should dates or questions of fact provoke discussion, there was always someone who insisted on going to the mataburros or "donkey-slayers" — that's what we called reference books.

The institution of factory readings made the tabaqueros into the most enlightened sector of the working class. The practice began in Cuba around 1864. . . . Emigrants to Key West and Tampa introduced the practice into the United States around 1869. . . . In Puerto Rico the practice spread with the development of cigar production, and it was Cubans and Puerto Ricans who brought it to New York. It is safe to say there were no factories with Hispanic cigarworkers without a reader. Things were different in English-speaking shops where, as far as I know, no such readings took place.[15]

Dennis Chávez

First Hispanic U.S. Senator

1888–1962

Dennis Chávez's roots lay deep in the dry, dusty soil of New Mexico. Born in Los Chávez— named after his ancestors—his family's ranchland could be traced back to a 1769 grant from the king of Spain. One of his relatives was the first *jefe politico*, or governor, of New Mexico after Spain ceded the territory to Mexico in 1821. More than a hundred years later, in 1935, Dennis Chávez, too, achieved a first when he became the first Hispanic member of the United States Senate.

The road Dennis Chávez took to his Senate seat was by no means an easy one. There were eight children in Dennis's family and his parents were desperately poor. Dennis completed the eighth grade and then dropped out of school to take a job driving a grocery wagon. Despite having to be at work early in the morning, Dennis read long into the night, usually the works of his favorite statesman, Thomas Jefferson. By the time he was seventeen, Dennis Chávez knew he wanted a career in government.

He knew, too, that to enter the field he would need more education. When, in 1916, he became the Spanish interpreter for New Mexico's U.S. Senator A. A. Jones and moved to Washington, D.C., he took the opportunity to enroll at Georgetown University. Because he had never attended high school, he had to pass a special exam before being admitted. Within a month, he passed the exam, enrolled at Georgetown, and began work as Senator Jones's legislative aide. Four years later, armed with a Georgetown University law degree and invaluable years of government experience, Dennis returned to Albuquerque to build his own political career.

Back home in New Mexico, he followed the classic pattern of America's elected officials. He first set up a law practice and then soon began campaigning for a seat in New Mexico's House of Representatives. He was elected easily and served many years in his home state before, in 1930, he ran for the U.S. House of Representatives.

Congressman Chávez served in the House four years before running for the Senate. In his first try in 1934, he lost a close, bitter race. A year later, however, when the new Senator, Bronson F. Cutting, was killed in a plane crash, Dennis Chávez was appointed to fill his seat. Senator Chávez was then elected in 1936 and held the seat for nearly thirty years, until his death in 1962.

Senator Chávez tried hard to help his constituents in New Mexico. He championed several causes that directly affected both Hispanics and Indians throughout the Southwest. As the Senate's only Hispanic member, he was eager to work against racial and ethnic discrimination. In the 1940s, after becoming alarmed at the miserable living conditions in Puerto Rico, he urged an investigation into the severe poverty of the island. One colleague nicknamed him "Puerto Rico's Senator" for his tireless efforts.

Fair employment and racial issues—both of great importance to Hispanics—brought Senator Chávez's work to the country's attention during the 1940s and 1950s. As a member of the Fair Employment Practice Committee, he lobbied hard to outlaw racial and religious discrimination in the workplace. As a member of the

Democratic National Committee, he struggled to force the party to address difficult racial issues in its platform.

New Mexico honored its senator by electing him again and again. Quiet and easy going, Dennis Chávez was a popular figure in his home state, where he was also famous for his nonstop cigar smoking. Like his poor but proud Spanish ancestors, one reporter wrote, he smoked "maybe a dozen a day . . . putting them down only to eat or legislate."

Senator Dennis Chávez died on November 19, 1962.

Carlos Castenada

Historian

1896–1958

When Carlos Castenada looked at the whole of American history, he saw not only the Pilgrims, the Revolutionary War, and the travels of Lewis and Clark, but also Coronado's expeditions, the founding of the California missions, and New Mexico's Pueblo Revolt of 1680. Professor Castenada, who taught history at the University of Texas at Austin from 1933 to 1958, felt that Spain and Mexico's influence on American history was of great importance. Mexican Americans, he believed, should be just as proud of their part in the development of the United States as the Anglo-Americans.

As he grew up in the border town of Brownsville, Texas, Carlos Castenada saw firsthand the sad plight of his fellow Mexican Americans. They wanted to be treated as equal citizens, but they were rejected by the Anglos. Mexicans had been in Texas for hundreds of years, but the Anglos would have the world believe their state's history began in 1836, when the Mexicans were defeated at the Alamo and the Lone Star State declared its independence.

Carlos Castenada graduated first in his high-school class and went on to the University of Texas to study engineering. At Austin, however, Carlos came under the spell of the famous historian, Eugene C. Barker, who taught the eager student to love the study of the past. It was a lesson Carlos never forgot.

> . . . I experienced the sheer joy of reconstructing the past from stray scraps, notes, letters, documents, those bits of men's minds and hearts that are traced in black and white on paper made frail by age. . . . It was fascinating and exciting; it got under my skin and into my blood.[16]

Carlos Castenada graduated with high honors in history from the University of Texas in 1921 and received his master's degree in 1923. Then, after teaching Spanish at Virginia's College of William and Mary for four years, he returned to the University of Texas and began his doctoral studies. He received his Ph.D. in 1932.

Professor Castenada was an optimist. The United States of America, he believed, was destined to lead the world because it had been founded by good, strong people. Castenada believed Spain's colonial empire brought culture and religion to the Indians and the mingling of Spanish influence with those of other European countries contributed to America's greatness.

Spanish-Mexican and Anglo-American history complement each other, he argued, and shouldn't be seen as one long trail of conflict. Each group has contributed to America's growth, and each must be proud of their own, and each other's, history. Professor Castenada urged his fellow Hispanics to look at their achievements and be proud.

Then how, many Texans asked the professor, do you explain the bloody Texas Revolution of 1836, when Santa Anna's forces clashed with Stephen A. Austin's? Wasn't that a conflict, from which followed even more conflict?

Professor Castenada urged Anglos and Mexicans to see the Texas Revolution in terms of good versus evil. Evil was represented by Santa Anna and his corrupt regime; both Mexican and American interests, he reasoned, were well served by defeating this tyrant.

His defeat was good for all Texans, both Anglo and Mexican.

Carlos Castenada encouraged interest in the field of Latin American studies. He urged his students to accept a Pan-American view of history; that is, the United States and Latin America share common origins and a common future. Their ties are stronger than their differences, and together they can ensure peace and democracy for the entire Western Hemisphere.

Many historians welcomed Castenada's Pan-Americanism. Others though, quibbled with his opinions. They felt his view of Spain's role in America's early history was too rosy. Didn't the Spanish church, some historians argued, bully the Indians and treat them like children? And, weren't many Spanish and Mexican rulers unspeakably cruel to both the Indians and to their own people? Does it serve anyone's purpose, they argued, to make the Spanish seem more benevolent than they really were?

Despite the controversy—or perhaps because of it—Professor Castenada brought the field of Latin American studies to life. He forced scholars and Mexican Americans to see the links between all Americans. His work led directly to the Chicano movement of the 1950s and 1960s and to increased political power for all Mexican Americans.

Jovita Mireles Gonzales

Historian, Folklorist

1904–

Jovita Gonzales's family was among the first settlers of Roma, Texas, which lies on the Rio Grande between Laredo and Brownsville. Jovita loved her native state and its Mexican heritage. She devoted her entire life to the study of *Tejanos* folklore and was one of the first to write in English about Mexican-American culture. She was a regular contributor to the *Annals* of the Texas Folklore Society and became the society's first Mexican-American president.

In the following excerpt, Jovita Gonzales writes lovingly about the lonely life of the *vaquero*, the Texas-Mexican cowboy who wandered freely over the cattle ranges of the huge state. Mrs. Gonzales observed with sadness that as large cattle companies bought up the rangeland, they erected barbed-wire fences. Fenced-in land meant the end of the wandering, free life of the *vaquero*.

> Texas born and Texas bred, [the *vaquero*] is considered even by many of those who know him—superficially—as an undesirable alien. He is a product of the state and loves Texas as his country; yet to Anglo-Americans of a few years' stay in the state he is an outcast. On one side, he descends from the first Americans, the Indians; on the other, his ancestry can be traced to the Spanish adventurer and conquistador. From the mingling of these two races a unique type has resulted.

. . . From his Indian ancestor he has inherited a love for freedom and the open prairie, a dislike for law and restraint . . . *"Suerte y Mortaja del cielo bajan"* ("Fortune and death come from above") seems to be his motto in life. . . .

From the Spaniard comes a courteous attitude toward women (especially before he is married), a daring spirit of adventure, and a deep-rooted love for beauty, particularly music and singing. From the same source he has also inherited a sincere religious feeling, which, mingled with pagan superstitions and beliefs, has added flavor and color to the legends and other forms of folklore of the borderland.

. . . An old vaquero told me once of what to him was paradise: the open prairies with no fences to hinder the roaming of the cattle and the wanderings of the cowboys. *"Cunado vino el alambre, vino el hambre."* ("With the coming of barbed wire came hunger.") . . . [T]he vaquero is a poet at heart. He sees the beauty of the sage brush in bloom; the singing of the mocking bird on clear moonlit nights invites him to sing—not songs of joy and happiness but plaintive melodies of unrequited love and tragedies. Like all people who live in close touch with Nature, he understands all the creatures of the woods and interprets them in his fanciful way. . . .

The folk-lore of the Mexican vaquero has the combined charm of the Andalusian lore as told by Fernan Caballero and the quaintness and simplicity of the Indian myth. To understand it is to understand the spirit and the soul of the Mexican people.[17]

The Braceros and the Mojados

Bracero is a Mexican term that comes from the Spanish word *brazo*, meaning "arm." In English, we might call a bracero a "hired hand." Twice during the twentieth century, braceros were brought into the United States—actually "hired" by the government—to help out in the agricultural and railroad industries. These workers were supervised by both the American and Mexican governments.

The first program began in August 1942 and ended late in 1947. The number of workers who entered the United States during this period was small, totaling no more than 250,000. The second period, which lasted from February 1948 to December 1964, was by far the longer and larger. During those sixteen years, 4.5 million Mexicans entered this country on temporary work permits.

Workers from Mexico had a great impact on the growth of the American Southwest even before World War II. In fact, workers had crossed the long border between Mexico and the United States since the beginning of the nineteenth century. Only in 1917, when the United States entered World War I, did the Mexican government ask American officials to help supervise the incoming farm workers. The Mexicans wanted the United States to provide workers such basic needs as housing, medical care, and sick pay. In return, they reasoned, American employers would get a steady supply of "good and cheap" labor. The United States, however, rejected the idea of any kind of formal arrangement.

The Mexican government was badly hurt when, during the Great Depression of the 1930s, American agriculture no longer needed foreign workers and let the Mexicans go. Because the laborers were not eligible for American relief, Mexico had to pay the high cost of taking thousands of impoverished men and women back into the country and trying to support them. A few years later, therefore, when the United States entered World War II, and fruit and vegetable growers again faced a shortage of American workers, the Mexican government refused to allow its workers to cross the border. American agricultural companies, desperate for seasonal farm workers, begged the government to enter into a bracero agreement. The U.S. and Mexican governments finally agreed on terms and the plan went into effect in 1942.

The first bracero program was considered a success. The Mexicans were good workers and eager to come into the United States. Wages were much higher here than in Mexico, and many families benefited by having at least one worker in the bracero program.

The typical bracero was a man in his mid-thirties, from either a small, remote village or a slum of one of Mexico's large cities. He usually couldn't read or write Spanish and spoke no English

at all. The bracero program offered him the only hope of supporting a large, extended family.

The bracero would stay in the United States, with one employer, for about six months. Then he would return home to his family and apply to come back for the next harvest season. Because American employers liked experienced employees, they would hire the same braceros year after year.

Despite the number of Mexicans who wanted to become braceros and the fact that American companies were happy with the arrangement, there were many critics of the program. Housing for workers was far below American standards. When the program first began, chicken coops and railcars were used to house workers. Finally, the government built camps, although these, too, provided only the most basic shelter. Many observers thought the fruit and vegetable growers were getting back more than they were giving.

After World War II, the bracero program ended, and there was no agreement between Mexico and the United States concerning migrant workers. After six months, the number of illegal workers or *mojados* ("wetbacks," so-called because they often entered the United States by crossing the Rio Grande River) increased dramatically. No one knows exactly how many mojados entered and reentered the country during this period. Most either had not been accepted into the bracero program or just wished to avoid government red tape. There were, unfortunately, many American growers willing to take the risk of hiring illegal workers just so they could pay them far lower wages than they would have to pay either braceros or American workers.

Southwestern fruit and vegetable growers lobbied long and hard for a new bracero program, and one finally went into effect in 1948. When the Korean War caused a new shortage of American workers,

Congress extended the program. After the war was over Congress extended it again, first for one year, then—at the urging of the growers—over and over.

Finally, by the 1960s, when it had become clear that the bracero program was the cause of poverty-level wages and terrible working conditions for Mexican-American workers, public opposition began to grow. Several congressional members pointed out that, in effect, the program was a subsidy to growers and worked against the interests of American farm workers, many of whom were Mexican Americans. Labor organizers accused the fruit and vegetable growers of using these foreign nationals to keep American unions out of agriculture.

In 1964, Congress at long last voted to end the bracero program. The way was now paved for union organizers to demand better working conditions for Mexican-American farm workers—which they did in very short order.

Braceros being taken to the fields to harvest crops.

The Ronstadts of Tucson

Frederico Ronstadt 1862–1954
Luisa Ronstadt Espinel 1892–1963
Linda Ronstadt 1946–

In 1933, at the peak of her career as a singer, dancer, and actress, Luisa Ronstadt Espinel looked back on her childhood in Tucson, Arizona. Her memories were filled with family picnics and long days and nights of music. ". . . [T]he moon shadows of the grape leaves latticed the arbor," she remembered, "and my father, sitting there, his face illumined, would accompany his songs on his guitar and later tell us marvelous stories of when he was a little boy. . . ."

Frederico Ronstadt, Luisa's father, had spent his childhood in Sonora, Mexico, where he was born in 1862. *His* father, an engineer from Germany, had come to the New World in 1850. He had married a Mexican woman and raised his family in the traditions of his adopted country. In 1882, sixteen-year-old Frederico Ronstadt left his family in Mexico and moved across the U.S. border into southern Arizona. Tucson was an especially welcoming place for Mexicans, and Fred eagerly accepted the frontier town's hospitality.

Fred Ronstadt's first job was as apprentice to the Southern Pacific Railroad. In 1888, when he was barely twenty, Fred started his own carriage business, which manufactured wagons, buggies, harnesses, and saddles. He quickly made his mark as one of the most astute businessmen in Tucson. As transportation needs changed—that is, as first steam engines plied their way across the desert and dusty plains and then as highways were built for cars and trucks—Fred did what was needed to keep his business growing. He was one of the few Arizona businessmen able to keep pace with the dizzying changes of the new century.

In 1919, one of Tucson's largest Spanish-language newspapers, *El Tucsonense*, ran a series of articles titled "Hombres de Empresa," about the leaders of the city's Mexican community. To no one's surprise, the first of these "men of enterprise," was Frederico Ronstadt, whose hardware and supply store, F. Ronstadt Company, was one of the largest in southern Arizona.

He told the *El Tucsonense* that when he was a teenager and new to Tucson, he dreamed of earning enough money so he could return to Mexico. But, as more family members joined him in Tucson, and as his business grew, he realized he would stay in Arizona his whole life. Still, he stated firmly, "not for a single moment did I forget my Mexican roots." His pride in being Mexican made him work hard at bringing the Anglo and Mexican communities together, as both friends and partners.

His love of Mexico included especially its music. In 1888, Frederico Ronstadt founded the Club Filarmónico. "We started out with eight or ten members," Fred recalled. "Some of them knew a little about music but the others didn't know a note. . . . We could have qualified for a circus burlesque, but in time we sounded better."

In time, in fact, they sounded so good that they became the leading orchestra in town. They played weekly concerts at the City Hall Plaza and various parks and were a staple of patriotic holidays like Memorial Day or the Fourth of July. The Club Filarmónico's greatest success came with a tour of Southern California. The band traveled on the Southern Pacific Railroad, giving well-attended concerts in Santa Barbara, Santa Monica, and Los Angeles.

Back in Tucson, the band gradually broke up as its members resumed their normal lives. Many, like Frederico, became successful businessmen and community leaders. Nevertheless, as Luisa Espinel remembered about her father and his music: "It was his whole life . . . his business was a secondary consideration."

Luisa Ronstadt was born in 1892, at the height of the Club Filarmónica's success. As a young woman, she appeared in local theater and musical productions, but at an early age, she knew her ambitions would take her far from Tucson. She studied first in San Francisco, then New York, Paris, and Madrid. She trained both as a classical musician and as a specialist in Hispanic folk music.

Luisa Ronstadt Espinel

Luisa traveled throughout the Spanish countryside, learning the songs and dances of the *paisanos*. The result of her travels were the beautifully created "Cuadros Castizos" or "typical pictures" of Spanish folklife. Wearing brightly colored costumes, Luisa performed her "pictures," around the world, teaching audiences about the way of life of Hispanic country people.

During the 1930s, Luisa Espinel appeared in several films including Josef von Sternberg's *The Devil Is a Woman*, also starring the great German actress Marlene Dietrich. In 1946, when her performing career was over and she was settled in Los Angeles, Luisa published a collection of Mexican folk songs. Many were passed down to her by Frederico Ronstadt, and so she called them *Canciones de mi Padre,* or *Songs of My Father.*

Frederico Ronstadt and his family

A mi padre con cariño—"to my father with affection"—she wrote in her introduction. "Those long summer evenings of my childhood, when the moon made strange patterns on father's guitar as he sang enchanting songs to me, are no more. . . ."

In 1988, Linda Ronstadt, one of the world's best-known singers of popular music, released an album that she, too, called *Canciones de mi Padre*, and she includes her Aunt Luisa's words as part of the introduction. Linda Ronstadt's father, Gilbert, was Luisa's brother; Frederico Ronstadt, whose Club Filarmónico first brought the sweet songs of Mexico and Spain to Tucson in 1888, was Linda's grand-father.

Linda Ronstadt was born in Tucson in 1946 and, like her Aunt Luisa, enjoyed a happy, family-filled childhood there. And, also like Luisa Espinel, her ambitions stretched far beyond southern Arizona. In 1964, Linda left Tucson for Los Angeles, and in 1967 she had her first hit song, "Different Drum," with her band, Stone Poney. It wasn't until the mid-1970s, however, that Linda Ronstadt emerged as one of the top female vocalists of the day. According to *Rolling Stone* magazine, Linda owed her success to "her looks, her charm, her ear for harmony, but above all to her voice, which is about the most versatile and strongest and most alluring vocal sound in pop music."

Linda Ronstadt has repeatedly challenged herself by recording many styles of music. When, in the late 1980s, she decided to make a record of Mexican songs, many fans—unaware of her Mexican heritage—thought she was yet again trying something new and exotic. Instead, some of the songs were so familiar that she re-members her father singing and playing them "during lazy Sunday afternoons" at the family's home in Tucson. In fact, the songs—*rancheras* and *huapangas* from the 1920s and 1930s—are, as she explains, "a tradition of my family . . . a living memory of heartfelt experience."

After *Canciones de mi Padre* was released in 1988, Linda Ronstadt began a concert tour. She created what she referred to as an old-fashioned evening of song and dance, something one might have seen in Mexico or the Southwest during the early 1900s. Something, perhaps, not so different from Luisa Espinel's "Cuadros Castizos"— or maybe even one of the Club Filarmónico's open-air concerts given on a long summer evening in Tucson, "when the moon made strange patterns on father's guitar. . . ."

Linda Ronstadt

José Arcadia Limón

Choreographer, Dancer
1908–1972

When José Limón was just twenty, he thought his career as an artist was over. He had wanted to be a painter and to work in the style of the great Spanish master, El Greco. But in that year, 1928, the passionate, mystical style of El Greco was completely out of fashion. Instead everyone wanted to copy the new, daring French painters. Thinking there was no place for him in the art world, José gave away his paints and brushes and stopped working altogether. He spent his days walking the streets of New York and sitting alone in movie houses.

José's friends became very worried. One evening, to try to boost his spirits, they took him to a modern dance recital. In 1928, modern dance was all the rage in New York, and several artists were capturing international attention. José sat completely still during the performance. At the end, he turned to one friend and said, "My God, *that's* what I want to do."

He immediately began taking classes with a well-known dancer and teacher, Doris Humphrey. A few months after seeing his first performance, José Limón made his own dance debut. He was, he later admitted, tense and lacking technique, but he had "found what he wanted." José Limón decided that he would be willing to stick with it.

By 1930, José was appearing in the first of many Broadway shows. He also began performing duets with Doris Humphrey and other partners. As José began choreographing his own dances, he drew from the Spanish *jotas* and Mexican *jarabes* he'd seen as a young boy in Culiacán, Mexico. Dancing, he recalled, "was part of the scenery of my childhood." These Hispanic dances suited his large build and his dark features, and they were very popular with New York and West Coast audiences.

World War II interrupted José's dance career. He joined the U.S. Army in 1942 and didn't dance seriously until the end of the war in 1945. He began performing publicly again in 1947 and received more critical praise than ever before. After seeing his performance of "Lament for Ignacio Sánchez Mejías," a *New York Times* critic wrote, "He is certainly the finest male dancer of his time. His appearance and bearing are magnificent." After seeing one of José's own compositions, "Moor's Pavane," in 1949, another critic said ". . . there is no other male dancer within even comparing distance of him."

When asked to describe how he approaches composition José Limón wrote, "I try to compose works that are involved with man's basic tragedy and the grandeur of his spirit. . . ." "I have limitations," he stated frankly. "Things don't come easily to me . . . I have to slug it out slowly and painfully. It takes me about three months to make a dance. Three months of daily brutal work."

José Limón taught dance at several colleges and universities, including Bennington College, Sarah Lawrence, the University of California, and the University of Pittsburgh. In 1950, the government of Mexico invited its native son to teach there regularly to revive, as they wrote, "the dance of Mexico along modern lines." José decided to spend several months each year in Mexico, where he quickly became a major celebrity.

In the early 1950s, the newly formed José Limón Dance Company was chosen by the U.S. State Department to tour Central and South America, Europe, and the Far East under its International Cultural Exchange Program. As audiences around the world saw his work firsthand, José's reputation grew.

During the 1960s, José Limón devoted himself to teaching and creating dances for his company. He rarely danced in public, although did give one last performance in 1969. José Limón died in 1972 at the age of 64. At the time of his death, *New York Times* dance critic Clive Barnes wrote that José was one "of America's greatest choreographers. . . . and as a dancer, an eagle."

Luis Alvarez
Physicist, Nobel Prize Winner
1911–1988

Luis wasn't the first—nor the last—scientist in the Alvarez family. In fact, there's hardly been a generation of Alvarezes that hasn't included a physician or a physicist or a geologist. Luis's father, Walter Alvarez, was a medical doctor who practiced at the famous Mayo Clinic and later wrote a health column that appeared in several large newspapers. *His* father, born in Cuba during the mid-1800s, arrived in the United States during the 1870s and then became a government physician for the kingdom of Hawaii. And now Luis's own son, Walter, is an eminent geologist who's caused a stir with his controversial ideas about dinosaurs.

So, perhaps no one was surprised when, in 1968, after a long, distinguished career, Luis Alvarez was given the Nobel Prize. Well, maybe *he* was, a little:

> On October 29, 1968, Jan and I attended a party. . . . The science editor of the *San Francisco Chronicle* introduced me there to his wife. "Oh, you're one of the Berkeley Nobel laureates," she said. I replied . . . that lots of my friends had won the prize but that I hadn't. That was the last time I had to apologize for not having won a Nobel Prize.
>
> At 3:30 the next morning the phone rang. When I answered it someone at CBS News in New York announced that word of my prize had just come over the wire from Stockholm. I asked with whom

I was to share it. It was all mine, he answered. My immediate reaction was . . . surprise.[18]

Luis was born in San Francisco in 1911. He attended public schools there and in Rochester, Minnesota. In 1928, he entered the University of Chicago; when he left Chicago in 1936 he had his doctoral degree in physics.

Dr. Alvarez began his teaching career at the University of California, Berkeley. War was on the horizon in Europe and before long he was sent by the government to the Massachusetts Institute of Technology to work on the development of radar, which was crucial to the war effort. While Luis was at the MIT Radiation Laboratory, he helped develop a radar beam so narrow that it could guide an aircraft, blinded by fog, to the ground. In 1944–45, Luis Alvarez went to Los Alamos, New Mexico, to work on the development of the atomic bomb. On August 6, 1945, Dr. Alvarez flew as a "scientific observer" in the B-29 *Great Artiste* as it followed the *Enola Gay* on its historic mission to Hiroshima, Japan. After the *Enola Gay* dropped the first atom bomb, he wrote: "We flew once around the mushroom cloud and then headed for Tinian. Japan looked peaceful from seven miles up."

That evening Luis Alvarez wrote a letter to his four-year-old son, Walter. It began:

> The story of our mission will probably be well known to everyone by the time you read this, but at the moment only the crews of our three B-29s and the unfortunate residents of the Hiroshima district in Japan are aware of what has happened to aerial warfare. . . . A single plane disguised as a friendly transport can now wipe out a city. . . . What regrets I have about being a party to killing and maiming thousands of Japanese civilians this morning are tempered with the hope that this terrible weapon we have created may bring the countries of the world together and prevent further wars. . . .[19]

After Japan's surrender and the end of World War II, Dr. Alvarez returned to Berkeley. The next twenty years of teaching and research were full and productive ones. The range of Luis's experiments was dazzling. As one colleague wrote, "He was the most imaginative, creative and inventive scientists I ever encountered. . . . He loved more than anything doing something that everyone else found impossible."

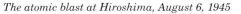

The atomic blast at Hiroshima, August 6, 1945

When the king of Sweden gave Luis Alvarez his Nobel Prize in 1968 he told the prestigious gathering that Dr. Alvarez's ". . . contributions to physics are numerous and important. Today our attention is focused on the outstanding discoveries which you have made in the field of high-energy physics as a result of your far-sighted and bold development of the hydrogen bubble chamber into an instrument of great power and precision and of the means of handling and analyzing the large quantities of valuable information which it can produce."

In 1980, Luis Alvarez joined with his son, geologist Walter Alvarez, in writing an article for *Science* magazine that proposed a new theory for why dinosaurs became extinct. The Alvarezes claimed, after careful experimentation, that they believed the cause to be extraterrestrial. About 65 million years ago, they wrote, a huge piece of rock from somewhere in the solar system hit the earth, throwing dust into the stratosphere that caused the sky to turn pitch black for several years. Because plants can't grow without light from the sun, all animal life eventually starved to death. This so-called impact theory, like any other theory in science, has its critics. The lively debate has taken its arguers into the realms of physics, geology, chemistry, paleontology, and astronomy. In the true spirit of scientific inquiry, Luis Alvarez said of controversy, ". . . only time will tell the real story."

Dr. Luis Alvarez died on September 1, 1988. The science world mourned the loss of the great physicist. One colleague called Luis that rare professional who ". . . seemed to care less about the way the picture in the puzzle would look when everything fit together than about the fun of looking for pieces that fit."

The American G.I. Forum

Hector Pérez García 1914–
Macario García 1920–
Physician, Civil Rights Organizer

Mexican Americans served bravely during World War II. Many men, who suffered from discrimination and underemployment in the United States, entered the U.S. Army, and made all Americans and other Chicanos proud. Unfortunately, when the fighting ended, veterans returned home to the same prejudice they'd left behind. Sergeant Macario García was only one of the decorated soldiers who faced humiliating conditions back home. In a book called *The Proud Peoples*, Harold J. Alford describes these men and what it was like for them when they returned.

> Sergeant Macario García . . . was visiting his parents, who were working in the beet fields at a place called Sugarland in his home state [of Texas]. He dropped into the Oasis Cafe for [a] cup of coffee and was greeted by the "We don't serve no Mexies in here" so familiar to members of La Raza wherever they went in the United States.
>
> "You'll serve me," Sergeant García said, "If I'm good enough to fight your war for you, I'm good enough for you to serve a cup of coffee to."
>
> . . . [The proprietor] grabbed Sergeant García by the collar and by the seat of the pants and was trying to swing him from the counter stool and head him toward the door.
>
> Two sailors were on their feet and coming over to try to stop the action. Three other customers were on their feet, too, coming from various directions toward the spot where the proprietor was still trying to unseat Sergeant García.

But before any of them could get there, the sergeant's combat-trained reflexes took over, and his left elbow dug into the proprietor's stomach. As García spun on the stool, the side of his right hand caught the proprietor on the point of the chin as he doubled forward from the punch to his stomach.

By that time, the other customers had arrived where the action was, and García found himself struggling against the . . . arms of two of them. Still another customer had grabbed the phone at the end of the counter and was busy dialing. For a brief time, the Oasis sounded more like a herd of stampeding Texas longhorns than a quiet cafe, and then the door burst open and a deputy sheriff charged in.

. . ."Look at that ribbon," one of the sailors told him. "It's the Congressional Medal of Honor. That's the highest decoration a guy can get, and anybody who's wearing it ought to be able to eat anywhere."[20]

President Truman presents Congressional Medal of Honor to Macario García

The sheriff ignored the ribbon and in order to "uphold the honor of the county," arrested Sergeant Macario García and charged him with "aggravated assault."

Word of the incident soon got out, and before long it was talked about from Mexico City to Washington, D.C. Famed radio personality Walter Winchell told his national audience about the insult to Sergeant Macario García. An angry nation wondered what can we do?

In Corpus Christi, Dr. Hector Pérez García was well acquainted with the insults endured by Mexican-American veterans. A distinguished combat surgeon, he believed strongly that prejudice and mistreatment should not be the lot of returning servicemen. Not only did most vets not receive benefits, but they weren't admitted to veterans' hospitals and couldn't find decent jobs.

The last straw came when, in 1948, a Texas undertaker refused to bury the remains of Felix Longoria, a Mexican-American soldier killed in the Battle of the Philippines. I don't work for Mexies, the undertaker had told the grieving family. President Harry S Truman was so upset by this incident that he arranged for Sergeant Longoria to be buried at Arlington National Cemetery in Washington, D.C.

The case of Felix Longoria caused Dr. García to vow such treatment of Mexican Americans wouldn't happen again—not if he could help it. In 1948, he organized the American G.I. Forum, whose mission was specifically to help Mexican-American veterans get the same services as other vets.

Dr. García, who was chairman of the board of the Forum, organized more than 100 chapters in Texas alone. Soon there were G.I. Forum members all over the country. By the 1950s, the group employed a full-time lobbyist in Washington, D.C.

Soon, the G.I. Forum moved beyond its original purpose of helping veterans and began speaking out on civil rights issues, hoping to encourage more understanding among all ethnic and religious groups. Dr. García also realized that Mexican-Americans needed to find their voice in America's political debate, so the Forum encouraged its members to work within their communites for political change. The G.I. Forum was soon recognized as an important Mexican-American organization.

Today, the American G.I. Forum is still going strong, with 20,000 members and 25 state and 500 local groups. Dr. García continues to lead the Forum and to make sure its mission ". . . to foster . . . the principles of American democracy based on religious and political freedom for the individual and equal opportunity for all" is carried out.

During the 1960s, Dr. García was appointed to a number of diplomatic posts and was made an alternate delegate to the United Nations. He became a member of the Civil Rights Commission and worked as a consultant to the Kennedy, Johnson, and Carter administrations. In 1984, Dr. García received the Presidential Medal of Freedom, America's highest civilian honor.

Dr. Hector Pérez García

Henry Barbosa Gonzales

Member, U.S. House of Representatives

1916–

Just five years before their son Henry was born, Leonides and Genevieve Gonzales moved from the state of Durango in Mexico across the Rio Grande to Texas. Leonides was a successful man—the mayor of his hometown—but by 1911, Mexico was in the midst of a bloody revolution and life for the Gonzaleses had become very difficult. Sadly, the family left their home, crossed the Rio Grande, and headed for San Antonio, Texas.

Leonides Gonzales was a hard worker who rose to managing editor of the Spanish-language newspaper, *La Prensa*. Still, there was often not enough money for food or clothing, and, so, young Henry was forced to work part-time. He worked while he attended elementary school, high school, and junior college in San Antonio. In 1936, he finally fulfilled his dream of moving to Austin to attend the University of Texas. However, in the midst of the Great Depression, jobs were so scarce that Henry couldn't support himself in Austin and was forced to drop out of the university. He returned home and finished his bachelor's and law degrees at St. Mary's University.

Henry's first job after leaving college was juvenile probation officer for Bexnar County, Texas. He eventually became the county's chief probation officer but quit when he was not allowed to hire a full-time black worker for his staff.

After working a variety of jobs that brought him in contact with the people of San Antonio, he was elected to the City Council in 1953. From then on, he devoted his life to politics and government, and he rose quickly. Henry Gonzales was elected to the Texas Senate in 1956, becoming the first Mexican American in the Texas Senate in more than one hundred years.

In 1961, he won a special election and went to Washington to fill out a term in the U.S. House of Representatives. Henry B. Gonzales thus became the first Mexican American from Texas ever elected to national office. The next year he was reelected, and he's served the people of San Antonio ever since.

Representative Gonzales has singled himself out as a champion of minorities. During his first ten years in Congress, he sponsored many bills supporting, among other things, basic adult education, Puerto Rican rights, minimum wage, and manpower training and development. Not surprisingly, he worked hard to defeat the long-term "bracero" bill, which gave government subsidies to temporary workers from Mexico. Many civil rights and labor activists were convinced the bracero program kept farm and factory wages earned by Mexican Americans too low. The bracero program, they believed, was one of the causes of the terrible poverty suffered by many laborers. The bill, with Representative Gonzales's help, was defeated in 1964.

Since that time, Congressman Gonzales has gained power in Congress while, in some ways, losing influence among Mexican-American organizations. In the heat of the Chicano rights movement, Henry Gonzales distanced himself from the leaders of La Causa, accusing them of "reverse racism." Many Mexican Americans have also noted a moderation in the congressman's liberal political views.

Representative Gonzales has served on such important House committees as Housing and Community Development and Banking, Finance, and Urban Affairs. Today, after thirty years in the House of Representatives, Henry B. Gonzales remains committed to issues of importance to all Hispanics.

Henry Gonzales was instrumental in working toward ending of the U.S. government's support of the Bracero program. This unidentified Mexican (below) was among the last to enter the United States in 1964 under the program.

Desi Arnaz

Band Leader, Actor,
Television Producer

1917–1986

When, in 1950, Desi Arnaz and Lucille Ball proposed to CBS-TV the idea for a half-hour comedy show based on the couple's own marriage, the response was nervous silence. True, Lucy and Desi were popular radio and stage personalities, but TV was different. Who would want to watch a show about a Cuban bandleader—who spoke English with a very thick accent—and his nutty red-headed wife?

The answer, of course, turned out to be "everyone."

When "I Love Lucy" was finally telecast in October 1951, it was an instant hit. For millions of American households, Monday became "Lucy" night—the time to stay at home and watch the crazy antics of Lucy and Ricky Ricardo.

Desi, who was christened Desiderio Alberto Arnaz y de Acha III, was born in Santiago, Cuba, in 1917. His father was the mayor of Santiago, and both the Arnaz and de Acha families were wealthy landowners. Desi could look back on a childhood spent riding horses around one of several family ranches or speeding along the island's coast in fast, sleek boats.

All that ended, though, in August 1933, when the Cuban Revolution overthrew the rule of President Gerardo Machado and his closest friends and advisers, including the Arnaz family. When the family's ranches and homes and stables were confiscated by the new government, the Arnazes fled to Miami, Florida. Suddenly poor, seventeen-year-old Desi earned money as a taxi and truck driver.

In 1934, Desi became a guitarist in one of Miami's many Cuban bands. Soon he began singing, too, and his winning stage personality caught the attention of the famous Spanish orchestra leader and rumba king, Xavier Cugat. Cugat invited Desi to join his orchestra as lead vocalist. After singing for a year with Xavier Cugat, Desi Arnaz returned to his own band, which played conga music—all the rage during the 1930s—in clubs throughout the United States.

By the end of the decade, Desi Arnaz was on his way to becoming a star. In 1939, he played a major role in a hit Broadway musical called "Too Many Girls." When the play was made into a movie, Desi agreed to recreate his Broadway role. His costar would be a bright, new Hollywood actress named Lucille Ball. The two met shortly after New Year's 1940 and were married less than a year later.

For the next ten years, Desi Arnaz and Lucille Ball worked hard at building their own careers. Desi traveled with his band, and Lucy acted in movies. They saw each other, they later estimated, a total of three years during the decade of the 1940s. They also spent approximately $30,000 on phone calls and telegrams, a very large sum of money for the day.

So, when in 1950, they formed Desilu Productions, it was partly to be able to finally work together. They created a comedy act— with Desi playing the straight-man bandleader and Lucy the scatterbrained wife—and set off on a national stage tour. The idea of a couple making fun of their own marriage was certainly not new, yet as audiences agreed, the Arnazes brought something fresh to this brand of humor. The freshness may have been partly due, as Lucy and Desi once told an interviewer, to the show being only a slight exaggeration of their real lives together.

When CBS-TV seemed reluctant to turn the comedy act into a television show, Desi and Lucy made a pilot with their own money and took it to the network's executives. CBS finally agreed the show could be a hit and signed a contract with Desilu. From the start the new husband-and-wife production company insisted on doing things their own way. Desilu wanted to make some basic changes in the way TV shows were made. At the time, half-hour shows were produced much like full-length movies—that is, they were filmed out of sequence and then put back together during the editing process. Desilu designed their shows as three-act plays and performed each one in sequence before a live audience. Both Desi and Lucy felt strongly that because TV was a livelier, more spontaneous medium than motion pictures, production methods needed to be adjusted to take advantage of the faster pace. They were, as history has proven, right on the money.

Long before "I Love Lucy," Desi Arnaz was a famous band leader and conga player.

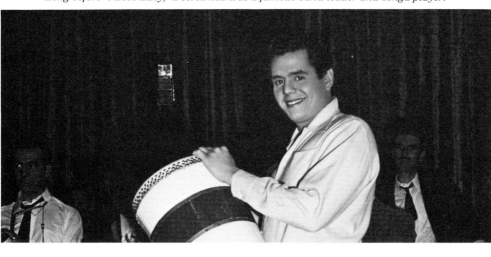

The plots of "I Love Lucy" are now familiar to generations of television viewers. Desi Arnaz plays Ricky Ricardo, the leader of a little-known Cuban band. Ricky speaks English with such a thick accent that sometimes even Lucy can hardly understand him. When Ricky is exasperated by Lucy—which is often—he speaks in rapid-fire Spanish. Lucy is delightfully off-center, amazing her husband and viewers each week with crazy schemes such as stealing an elephant or setting fire to Ricky's newspaper so he'll notice her at the breakfast table. Their amazing worldwide popularity was at least partly due to the fact that, as one reviewer wrote, they managed to "convince viewers that *any* wife might buy $700 worth of meat for a deep freezer or glue a beard on her face in a campaign against her husband's mustache."

During the 1950s, while Desi and Lucy were filming the weekly "I Love Lucy" episodes, Desilu Productions was branching out and becoming a very large company. They produced such other landmark shows as "The Untouchables," "Our Miss Brooks," and "The Danny Thomas Show."

"I Love Lucy" ran for eleven seasons, from 1951–1961. Unfortunately, the day-to-day stresses of starring and producing in one hit TV show, while producing several others, strained the Arnazes' marriage. In 1960, Lucille Ball and Desi Arnaz were divorced.

By 1962, Desi Arnaz made the decision to retire from television. He sold his stock in Desilu Productions to Lucille Ball and moved to his horse ranch in Del Mar, California. He ventured north to Hollywood a few times after his retirement but, for the most part, lived away from show business's bright lights. He died in 1986 at the age of sixty-six.

Gregory Rabassa

Translator

1922–

Even though Gregory Rabassa's father was born in Cuba, he didn't encourage his son to learn Spanish. Gregory's father, like many ambitious immigrants, wanted to rush ahead with his new life and let go of the old. So, it wasn't until Gregory attended New Hampshire's Dartmouth College that he began to study his father's native language. And even then, it seemed very unlikely that, one day, Gregory Rabassa would become the translator of many of Latin America's greatest Spanish-language writers, including Nobel Prize–winners Gabriel García Márquez and Octavio Paz.

Immediately after graduating from Dartmouth, Rabassa served in World War II, working in North Africa and Italy with the Office of Strategic Services. His first job as a translator included receiving and reworking military codes—something very different from the work that would eventually make him famous. When the war ended, Gregory Rabassa began graduate studies in Spanish at Columbia University in New York City. After receiving his doctoral degree, he taught and—in whatever spare time his faculty duties left him— translated.

Gregory Rabassa's entry into the field of translation in the early 1960s coincided with a new golden age in Latin American literature. In many countries of Central and South America, previously unknown authors were publishing stunning, challenging new works. Among these talents were Julio Cortázar of Argentina, Gabriel García Márquez of Colombia, Mario Vargas Llosa of Peru, and Octavio Paz of Mexico. During the 1960s and 1970s, Professor Rabassa translated the novels of all these great writers. In fact, one of the reasons why García Márquez's 1967 novel, *Cien Años de Soledad*, was not published in English until 1970 was that Julio Cortázar had advised the Colombian novelist to have it translated by Gregory Rabassa and no one other. García Márquez took this advice and, in effect, got in line for the translator's service. The final product, *One Hundred Years of Solitude*, found a huge audience and left large numbers

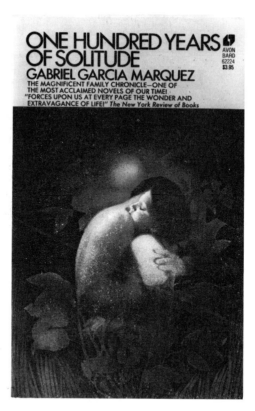

of readers worldwide hungry for more works by these talented Latin American writers.

Gregory Rabassa, however, is modest about his contribution to the success of the works he translates. Their greatness, he insists, is a product of the skill of their creators. Before such men as, first, Argentina's Jorge Luis Borges and later García Márquez began publishing their original, brilliant works, Latin American literature was considered a weak imitation of its Spanish and European counterparts. These writers, finally, brought their unique Latin American landscape to life.

In fact, Gregory Rabassa views his role as that of a middleman and, as such, he travels frequently to Latin America searching for new literary talent. "It is easier to get published down there than it is in the U.S.," Rabassa told *Time* magazine in 1988, but harder to make money at it. With Rabassa's golden touch, little-known, struggling writers have become international literary celebrities.

Now, as he approaches his seventieth birthday, Rabassa still devotes most of his time to sampling this hemisphere's Spanish-language literary treats and offering them to eager consumers. He is confident that the originality—many call it magic—of Latin American literary artists will continue to challenge and entertain the world for many years to come.

César Chávez

Chicano Leader, Founder of the United Farm Workers

1927–

No one had to tell César Chávez what it was like to be a migrant farm worker. He knew from long, bitter experience that it was a miserable way to live. In fact, it could just barely be called "living" at all; "surviving" was closer to the truth.

When César was born in Yuma, Arizona, the Chávez family were farm *owners*. His grandfather, a runaway slave from Chihuahua, Mexico, had acquired farmland near the Gila River at the end of the nineteenth century. Grandfather Chávez enjoyed the sight of his children and his children's children working side by side in the fields, growing food for their own table.

One day in 1937 during the Great Depression, when César was ten years old, his family learned that, because they didn't have enough money to pay Arizona's property taxes, they would have to give up their farm. Their neighbors, too, were losing old family farms. In fact, families across the country were finding themselves in similar situations. There was simply not enough money to pay the necessary bills. All the Mexican farmers in Yuma wondered where they would find food and shelter for their families.

Soon after the Chávez family learned that they would lose their farm, labor contractors paid them a visit. Large farms in Arizona and California, the Chávezes were told, needed workers. If the family was willing to travel several hundred miles north with the contractors, they could all earn a good living. They wouldn't just work at one farm but at several different ones, moving as the seasons changed.

The Chávez family was sad to leave Yuma but excited about the prospect of earning more money. César's parents thought that at last they could save enough to educate their children. When, after a long, hot ride in the back of a pickup truck, they reached the first farm in California's Imperial Valley, they were terribly disappointed and afraid. The only place for them to live was a one-room shack made out of sheet metal. There was no running water and only a single gas burner for cooking.

Migrant farm work was not at all like what had been promised. The Chávez family earned less money, not more, and both their living and working conditions grew worse. All ages were expected to stay out in the hot fields from dawn till dusk, doing "stoop labor." What's more, they traveled so often—from Arizona to the Imperial Valley of California to as far north as the San Joaquin Valley— that schooling for the children was very haphazard. By the time César finished eighth grade—his last year of formal education— he'd been in thirty-six different schools!

When César was still a teenager, he left his family's itinerant life and got a job of his own. He chose to work in the vineyards near Delano, California, pruning and training the grapevines and then picking the grapes during harvest. Before long, he married and then, when World War II began, he joined the Navy.

When the war ended and the Mexican-American farm workers returned to California, César was determined that conditions would improve. Why had all these men given so much for their country during wartime, he asked, if only to come back and be treated like second-class citizens? César immediately began organizing to improve both living and working conditions for Mexican-American farm workers.

When, inevitably, César Chávez was fired from his job, he took a new one with the Community Service Organization (CSO). The CSO helped farm workers and other poor people by finding them housing, medical care, legal services, and many of life's necessities. It also helped Mexican Americans register to vote so they could begin to exercise their rights as U.S. citizens.

Through his work with the CSO, César Chávez came to believe that farm workers would remain powerless unless they had their own union. On September 30, 1962, he founded the National Farm Workers Association (NFWA) in Fresno, California.

At first, it was very difficult convincing farm workers to join the new union. Many of the growers bullied their employees and threatened to fire them if they joined. César traveled throughout the grapefields of California trying to convince workers of the benefits of union membership. Of course, you're afraid of your Anglo bosses, he said, but with our help you can stand up to them and get the wages and working conditions you deserve.

The National Farm Workers Association grew until, finally, in 1965, they felt powerful enough to demand pay raises from the three largest California grape growers. They asked that their wages be raised to $1.40 per hour and that they be given an additional 25¢ for each box they picked. When the growers refused, the cry of *Huelga*—Strike!—rang out from the corners of the vineyards. The workers knew that if no one picked the grapes, the harvest would be ruined. Two of the grape growers agreed to allow their farm workers to join the union, but a third—Giumarra Vineyards, the nation's largest producer of table grapes—held out, and the strike went on.

At the Giumarra fields, truckloads of contract workers were brought in from Mexico to pick the grapes. The striking workers shouted for the Mexicans to honor the strike, but the Mexicans were too afraid not to do as they were told by the growers. In the meantime, the story of César Chávez and his workers' union became well-known all over the country. The fledgling union started to receive money and goods from sympathetic organizations and individuals.

César Chávez addresses a crowd of people during his boycott of table grapes

The support shown the National Farm Workers Association gave César Chávez the idea of starting a boycott. Farm workers and volunteers around the country asked Americans not to buy California grapes unless they carried the union label.

César Chávez received well-publicized support from Martin Luther King, Jr., Robert Kennedy, and even Pope Paul VI. He organized rallies, marches, and hunger strikes, all bringing the country's attention to the plight of the Mexican-American farm worker. Still, back in Delano, the strike dragged on into its fourth year. As César told rallies across the country:

> Our strikers have been under the gun, they have been kicked and beaten and herded by dogs, they have been cursed and ridiculed, they have been stripped and chained and jailed, they have been sprayed with the poisons used in the vineyards. . . . But they have been taught not to lie down and die nor to flee in shame, but to resist with every ounce of human endurance and spirit. [21]

Finally, in 1970, Giumarra and most of the other California table-grape growers agreed to the union contract. In 1972, the NFWA became the United Farm Workers and a member union of the AFL-CIO.

Today, César Chávez, a grandfather several times over, continues his work in Delano, California. Conditions have improved but the struggle continues.

Rubén Salazar

Journalist
1928–1970

"Justice is the most important word in race relations. Yet too many Mexican Americans in the Southwest feel that to Anglos justice means 'just us.'"

from *Strangers in One's Land*

At first glance, Rubén Salazar would seem an unlikely political martyr. At the time of his death, Rubén was a successful newspaper columnist and television executive. Married to an Anglo, he and his wife lived with their three children in conservative Orange County, California. Yet in the fall of 1970, the name "Rubén Salazar" became a rallying cry for all those seeking true justice for Mexican Americans.

Rubén Salazar was born in Juárez, Mexico, but moved with his family to Southern California when he was still a boy. He learned English quickly and became so skilled at reading and writing his second language that in 1959, he became a reporter for the *Los Angeles Times*.

In the early 1960s, Rubén became the *Times*'s correspondent in the Dominican Republic and Vietnam. Later he was named chief of the paper's Mexico City bureau. In 1968, he returned to Los Angeles and in 1969, just as he announced plans to leave the *Times* and become news director of Spanish language television station KMEX, he was chosen by the *Times* to write a weekly column on Chicano issues. According to the *Times*'s editor in chief, James

Bassett, Rubén's job would be to "close an information gap" that existed between Los Angeles's Mexican and Anglo communities.

Rubén Salazar took on both jobs—news director *and* weekly columnist—with great energy. The column became nationally recognized for its tough approach to questions of poverty, discrimination, and racism.

One week, Rubén advocated substituting "Chicano" for "Mexican American." The term "Chicano," he said was an "act of defiance and badge of honor for activists." In other columns, he "informed" *Times* readers about the miserable living conditions in much of the Chicano community. When, in June 1970, *Newsweek* magazine asked Rubén about his approach to the column, he replied: "Bassett keeps telling me to explain the Chicano to the white community, but more important things keep coming up. When you've been a reporter this long, you go for more significant, hard-hitting stuff than telling why people eat enchiladas."

By August 1970, there was even more hard news to report. The Chicano community in East Los Angeles, reflecting the general mood of the country, was tense and restless. As the Vietnam War dragged on, and a great number of Hispanic surnames appeared on the casualty lists, Chicano leaders began to stage street demonstrations. Young Mexican Americans began scuffling regularly with members of a nervous Los Angeles Police Department.

On August 29, the situation took a turn for the worse. That date had been set by Chicano leaders as the Chicano National Moratorium on Vietnam. A rally was organized, and as nearly 100,000 people gathered in East Los Angeles's Laguna Park to protest Chicano involvement in the war, tensions between protesters and the police began to grow. In the middle of the afternoon, after reports of some looting, the police arrived in full riot gear. They quickly became the target for rocks and bottles thrown by the protesters. Shots were fired and several arrests were made.

About five o'clock that afternoon, Rubén Salazar, covering the event for KMEX, ducked into Laguna Park's Silver Dollar Bar with a few coworkers. The bar was quiet inside, but all around it police tried to control the huge crowd. According to one report, sheriff's deputies looking "for someone with a rifle" surrounded the bar. They yelled into the Silver Dollar that everyone should leave immediately, but before giving the patrons a chance to exit, fired three high-speed tear gas projectiles into the bar. One hit Rubén Salazar in the head and killed him instantly.

A burning car litters a Los Angeles street in the aftermath of the riot that killed Rubén Salazar.

In the days that followed Rubén's death, the Chicano community, and indeed the entire country, tried to grapple with the facts. Many accused the police of deliberately murdering the journalist. The police, it was learned, had told Rubén repeatedly to tone down his reports on the community. Many newspapers throughout the United States and Mexico jumped in to vent their opinions about the riots and the death of Rubén Salazar.

An inquest into his death began on September 10, 1970, and lasted sixteen days. In the end, after 2,025 pages of testimony from 61 witnesses, nothing was settled. Of the seven-member coroner's jury, four believed the death was "at the hands of another" and three thought it was accidental. Many wanted someone in the police department tried for murder but no such action was ever taken.

Rubén Salazar's voice for orderly social change was sorely missed. He had been calm, articulate, and very knowledgeable about both the Chicano and Anglo communities. He was a bridge builder, trying to bring the two reluctant sides together. After his death, the bridge seemed ready to crumble.

Richard "Pancho" Gonzales

Tennis Champion

1928–

That first racket of mine, to me, was the eighth wonder of the world. . . . I never let it out of my sight. I took it to bed with me to protect the strings and a warping frame from the temperature changes of the room.

To find the proper grip . . . I shook hands with it all day, more often than a politician pumps the hands of prospective voters. Sometimes I even talked to it.

I'd say, "Good morning, Señor Tennis Racket."

And in my own falsetto, the racket would reply, "Good morning, Señor Gonzales."[22]

Pancho was, to say the least, an unlikely tennis champion. At a time when tennis was still a gentleman's sport played mostly at private clubs, Pancho stunned tennis fans by scrapping his way to the top with the feisty determination of a boxer.

Born in Los Angeles to Mexican-born parents, Pancho was the first in the Gonzales family to play tennis. But Pancho was, as he admits in his autobiography, a wild kid with more restless energy than his parents could handle. Sitting still was impossible for him; he always wanted to be on the move—usually to somewhere he shouldn't go. As he recalled in his autobiography, when he told his mother he very badly wanted a bike, his mother said, "'Too dangerous. I'll get something safer.' She went to the May Company and bought me a tennis racket."

Pancho took the racket to a public tennis court a few blocks away and began hitting a beat-up ball he found lying on the ground. From that moment on, as he remembers, "I was madly in love." Tennis became his life.

Still, he never took formal lessons. Instead he learned by watching and practicing. And he won by hitting the ball harder than anyone else—especially on his serve—and moving faster, and more skillfully, than most. He won his first tournament in 1939, while still in junior high. That same year the *Los Angeles Times* sports editor wrote a column titled "Southern California—Cradle of Tennis Champions." Eleven-year old Pancho Gonzales was mentioned prominently. The young player won several more tournaments before dropping out of school and joining the amateur tennis tour.

He rose steadily in the amateur ranks, but in 1945 took time off to serve in the U.S. Navy. He didn't play tennis seriously again until 1947, when he finished the year ranked number seventeen in the country. As the 1948 season got under way, *American Lawn Tennis* magazine wrote: "It is our opinion that the six-foot-three powerhouse from Los Angeles is one year away from the top." As it turned out they were right. Pancho improved steadily throughout the summer, and in September he won the U.S. Singles Championship at Forest Hills.

His stunning success came with a price, though. Pancho himself admits his head was turned by all the acclaim and attention he received after winning Forest Hills. In 1949, he trained poorly, gained weight, and lost his edge. Sports writers began calling him "the problem child of tennis." As he battled with both the media and himself, he began to lose crucial matches, so that, only a year after his victory, no one expected him to win at Forest Hills again. They expected Pancho Gonzales to prove what many sports writers had said all along—that his victory in 1948 had been a "fluke."

But, just as he'd done the year before, Pancho buckled down. He declined invitations to parties and social events and concentrated instead on his tennis. And, when the prestigious tournament was over, he was again the men's singles champion. His favorite part about winning for the second year, he recalls, was seeing the next cover of *American Lawn Tennis*. There he was, smiling broadly with his wife Henrietta at his side. The caption reads: The Last Laugh.

Pancho Gonzales turned professional the next year. Because it wasn't until 1968 that Open tennis began—that is, when the major Grand-Slam tournaments could be played by both professionals and amateurs—professional players couldn't compete at Wimbledon, Forest Hills, and Paris. They could earn a lot of money, which was important for a player who, like Pancho, had a wife and three children. Pancho's professional career got off to a slow start but by 1954, he was the world Professional Singles Champion and held onto that title until 1961.

Even after 1961, Pancho Gonzales continued to be ranked among the top ten players of men's tennis. In 1972—24 years after his first singles title—he was still ranked as high as number nine. He had truly won the right to be considered one of the game's greatest players.

Pancho Gonzales still plays in senior's events, mostly "just for fun." During most of his retirement though he works as a teaching pro in Los Angeles.

Marisol

Sculptor

1930–

The way Marisol (from the Spanish words for "sea and sun"—*mar y sol*) approaches her art is anything but usual. An early morning near her home in New York City might find her, accompanied by her big, shaggy dog, pushing an old cart, prowling through the debris of a ruined building. She'll search through the rocks and clumps of wood and often find a worker to help her turn over or move an old wooden beam. She'll load her treasures, and then wheel them back to her studio, where she'll use a hammer, a chisel, and various electric tools to work the pieces into the figurines that she's become internationally known for.

Marisol Escobar was born in Paris to a wealthy family from Venezuela. She spent most of her youth traveling, ". . . always traveling, my brother and I, with suitcases and trunks, and staying in hotels." Her family would return to Venezuela from time to time but she never thought of that country as "home." As she looks back on her youth she realizes that, in fact, she never had a home; art has been her only "safe haven."

Marisol moved to New York City when she was nineteen and studied at the Art Student's League. She'd long been interested in Pre-Columbian art—that is, the art of the Aztecs and Mayan and other Indians of Central and South America—and she made her first wood and clay figurines to imitate this style. As her artistic vision grew, her work came to be seen as a cross between popular art and folk art.

Art lovers soon viewed Marisol as a witty, inventive sculptor. Her quirky pieces attracted much attention, especially during the 1950s and 1960s, when the public seemed to crave slightly eccentric personalities. Marisol worked with great seriousness and purpose, but her public personality was a little zany. Once she showed up for a panel discussion at New York's Museum of Modern Art wearing a white Japanese mask. She kept the mask on throughout the evening, until finally the audience clamored for her to take it off. When Marisol did remove the mask, her face was made up to look exactly like the mask.

In addition to her figurines, Marisol has created many large sculptures. One, "The Party," features thirteen partygoers all wearing bits and pieces of Marisol's own clothes and all bearing her face. Another sculpture, which has been exhibited in museums around the world, but which Marisol still keeps in her personal possession, is "My Mama y Yo." This features a young child holding up a parasol to protect her lovely mother. Marisol's own mother died when the artist was very young, and the work seems to depict a child's attempt to shield her frail mother from harm.

Her work has found homes in the world's greatest museums— in New York alone her pieces are in the collections of the Museum of Modern Art, the Whitney Museum of American Art, and The Metropolitan Museum. Now she spends all her time in New York, working and sleeping, as she says. She stays put not because of her age, but because she's sees no need to travel. Things always change right here, she states happily. If I need a change of scene, I just go to a cafe down the street.

Marisol feels that a lifetime of art has given her freedom. Freedom to join or not join as she chooses; to travel or not. It's a freedom that finds joy in the smallest things—such as, exploring the rubble of an old building.

The Family. *(1962) by Marisol. Painted wood and other materials in three sections, overall, 6' 10 ⁵/₈ " x 65 ¹/₂" x 15 ¹/₂'. Collection, The Museum of Modern Art, New York. Advisory Committee Fund.*

Rita Moreno

Actress, Singer, Dancer
1931–

Shortly after five-year-old Rosa Dolores Alverio arrived in New York City from Puerto Rico, she began taking dancing lessons. Rosa's mother, Rosa Maria, had to work long hours as a seamstress to pay for them. But what else could she do? Everyone said Rosita was so talented. Maybe, Rosa Maria hoped, she can sing and dance her way out of the slums of New York.

Soon, in fact, Rosita Alverio was able to earn some money as a child performer. She appeared at Macy's Department Store and often performed at weddings and bar mitzvahs. Usually, she was asked to wear wildly colored costumes, wear bananas on her head, and sing and dance just like the very popular Brazilian singer Carmen Miranda.

Rosita had no way of knowing that, years later, when she was on her own and using the stage name, Rita Moreno, she'd often feel that audiences still only wanted her to act like some other Latin star, but never just herself. Latin women are fiery and temperamental and so that's how you, too, must be, producers and directors would tell her. While still in her teens Rosita appeared first on Broadway and then in nightclub shows. I do have the talent, she tried to convince herself, if only people would let me use it.

In Hollywood, during the late 1940s and 1950s, she was under contract first with MGM, then 20th Century Fox. Always, in movie after movie, she portrayed the kind of woman she herself referred to as "Rita the Cheetah." In one western, called *Seven Cities of Gold*, she played a Mexican woman who asks a U.S. soldier "Why joo no luv Oola no more?" and when she hears his answer, jumps off a cliff.

The only time she wasn't playing a doomed Latin, she was cast as an Arab or an Indian. In Hollywood, exotic meant a dark face —no one was too particular about the details.

Despite her disappointment with the roles offered her, Rita Moreno always worked hard. She also moved easily from the stage to nightclubs to film to television and back again. Critics raved about her performances and urged Hollywood and Broadway producers to let her try more challenging parts—real drama, real dancing, and singing, where Rita could show her great talent.

In 1956, Rita played a supporting role in the film adaptation of the hit musical *The King and I*. For the film's ballet sequence, she worked with the great choreographer, Jerome Robbins. Their work together was so successful that a year later he suggested she try out for the lead in a new musical he was choreographing, "West Side Story." It was an updated version of "Romeo and Juliet," set in Spanish Harlem and featuring two warring street gangs. Regretfully she declined, telling Mr. Robbins, she simply had too many other commitments.

Jerome Robbins didn't forget Rita Moreno, though, and, in 1960, he cast her in the film version of *West Side Story*. This time she wasn't asked to play the lead character named Maria—that role would go to Natalie Wood—but Anita, Maria's cousin. Rita did all her own singing for the part and worked long hours with Mr. Robbins on the dance numbers, especially the famous "America." The film won ten Academy Awards, including one for Rita Moreno as Best Supporting Actress.

During the 1970s, Rita Moreno received many more honors, eventually becoming the only performer to win all four of the entertainment world's most important awards—the Oscar for films, the Emmy for television, the Tony for the Broadway stage, and the Grammy for a recording. She won a Grammy in 1972 for a soundtrack recording of the PBS show "The Electric Company." Her two Emmy Awards came for guest appearances on "The Muppet Show" in 1977 and "The Rockford Files" in 1978.

Her Tony Award came in a comedy role in the play "The Ritz," which opened on Broadway in 1975. She played a Puerto Rican singer named Googie Gómez, whose ambitions go far beyond her talent. The critics, as they say, raved about the outrageously funny performance. ". . . [S]he tears the house down every time she opens her mouth," one wrote. "She is showing a new generation of theatregoers what stars are all about." Rita especially enjoyed the Tony Award because she saw the role of the wild Googie Gómez as a way of getting back at all the writers and producers who only wanted to see her as "Rita the Cheetah."

Rita Moreno continues to appear regularly on stage, screen, and television. When not working, she lives quietly with her husband, a cardiologist, in New York City.

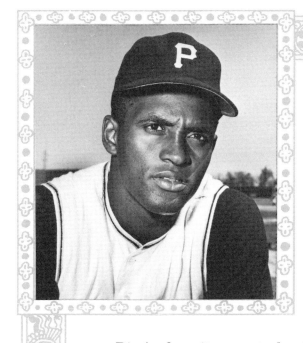

Roberto Clemente

Baseball Player

1934–1972

Baseballs were expensive in Puerto Rico during the 1930s; a poor sugar-cane worker like Melchor Clemente would never have been able to afford one. So when Melchor's son, Roberto, wanted to play Puerto Rico's favorite sport, he had to make his own baseball. He first scouted around his hometown of Carolina for a beat-up golf ball. Then he removed the string from burlap dried bean and rice bags and wrapped it around the hard ball many times. When he put a final layer of tape around the many layers of string, Roberto took his "new" ball to the hilly clearing where his friends gathered to play.

In those early days, no one thought Roberto would amount to much as a baseball player. He was so small and thin that he didn't have the strength to hit or throw hard. His small hands could just barely go around the big, clumsy string ball. I'll never be big enough to hit that ball very far, he complained to himself often.

By the time Roberto Clemente entered high school, though, he was no longer a puny kid. He was muscular and beautifully co-ordinated. He was the fastest runner in Carolina and could throw anything—a javelin, a baseball—with awesome speed and accuracy. Many were already beginning to use the word "great" with Roberto's name.

In 1954, scouts from the Brooklyn Dodgers came to Puerto Rico looking for new baseball talent. At the Sixto Escobar Stadium in the San Juan suburb of Santurce, scout Alex Campanis asked seventy-two hopeful players to take turns fielding, pitching, and batting. Mr. Campanis watched the players closely. "How could I miss him?" he said later, referring to eighteen-year-old Roberto Clemente. "He was the greatest natural athlete I have ever seen. . . ." After sorting through the major-league offers that year, Roberto signed with the Dodgers and headed into the cold North.

He was, he quickly admitted, a little scared. He knew the American major leagues were full of talent and that a player from Puerto Rico would have to go a long way to prove himself. He was worried, too, about the color barrier. Roberto was black, and it had only been seven years since Jackie Robinson had become the first black man to play in the major leagues. How would he—a black man who spoke only a little English—fare?

But Roberto was also happy to be living his dream. The Dodgers had already paid him more money than his father could earn in the sugar-cane fields in years, and he hadn't even put on their uniform yet. He could, he knew, become somebody. It would just take hard work and fierce determination, and he knew he could deliver both.

Despite Jackie Robinson's break through though, baseball teams still had informal quota systems. Blacks were so new to the major leagues that club owners worried fans would turn away from their favorite teams if they became too black. The Brooklyn Dodgers already had four blacks, and even though they desperately wanted Roberto Clemente, they felt major-league baseball wasn't ready for an all-black outfield. So they put Roberto "on hold" by sending him to their minor-league farm team in Montreal.

Roberto might not have minded a stint in the minor leagues were it not for the fact that the Dodgers didn't intend to train him in Montreal but hide him—hide him from other scouts who would steal him away for another team. He was too good for the minors, the Dodgers knew, but they just couldn't put him on the starting roster, not yet. The only problem was that Roberto didn't know why he wasn't being allowed to play to his capacity, and he became confused and angry. Finally, when Al Campanis came to Montreal to see his recruit, Roberto poured out his frustrations: "I want to go home. . . . I know I can play better than these guys, but I am not being used!"

Al Campanis urged Roberto to be patient and remember that he had a long career ahead of him. Meanwhile, a scout from the Pittsburgh Pirates spotted Roberto in practice and urged his team to sign him as soon as possible. At the end of the 1954 season, the team decided to sign the impressive outfielder. Roberto was back home in Puerto Rico for the winter when he heard the news. "I didn't even know where Pittsburgh was," he later admitted.

Roberto Clemente was a popular player for the Pittsburgh Pirates right from the start. In 1955, the last-place Pirates didn't have much to cheer about, but they did cheer for Roberto Clemente. They loved the way he caught the ball with both feet off the ground and then whirled around to make an on-target throw. He was also an excellent hitter and had a batting average of close to .300 by his second season.

By 1960, the Pittsburgh Pirates were a strong enough team to play the New York Yankees in the World Series. The Series went to seven games, with Roberto getting at least one hit in each. The Pirates won the seventh game and the Series.

From then on there was no question, Roberto Clemente was a star. He won four National League batting championships and played in the All-Star game nearly every year. Still, there were many times he felt unhappy and unsettled. He longed for the off season when he could return to his home in Puerto Rico.

Back home in 1964 he met Vera Zabala and within a year they were married. Vera seemed to add the security and happiness that was missing from Roberto's life. The couple eventually had three sons. They built a house in Río Piedras, Puerto Rico, near Carolina, where Roberto relaxed and entertained his many friends.

Each spring he returned refreshed to Pittsburgh and to the Pirates. In 1971, the team won another league championship and played the Baltimore Orioles in the World Series. To many baseball fans, Roberto's performance during the Series surpassed even what they had come to expect from such a fine player. Just like the 1960 Series, this one came down to the seventh and deciding game. The Pirates, plagued by injuries and with weak pitching, didn't seem to have a chance of winning this game, which was to be played in front of 47,000 screaming Baltimore fans.

As millions watched around the world, Roberto hit a home run in the fourth inning. Only two more runs were scored during the entire game, and the Pirates won, 2-1. Roberto, at the age of thirty-seven and with fifteen seasons of Major League baseball behind him, was named the Series Most Valuable Player. His joy in playing and the enthusiasm of the fans convinced him not to retire.

His main hope for the 1972 season was to hit his 3,000th hit, and thereby join the ten other players in baseball history who reached this milestone. This hitting award was very important to Roberto, partly because, as he told an interviewer that year, ". . . it means that I didn't fail with the ability I had."

The historic hit came in a game against the New York Mets on September 30, 1972. A few weeks later, the season was over.

The Pirates made it to the National League playoffs but eventually lost to the Cincinnati Reds. Roberto, as usual, headed home to his family in Puerto Rico. He planned to spend the winter thinking about whether or not to retire. He loved baseball but had so many new dreams he wanted to see through. He wanted to found a sports complex in Puerto Rico, help upcoming Latin ball players, perhaps start a business.

In December 1972, the terrible news of an earthquake in Managua, Nicaragua, dimmed the Christmas season. Many people were killed or left homeless. Relief aid from all over the world was sent to the victims of the small Central American nation.

Roberto asked his friends in Puerto Rico to donate food, medicine, and other supplies, and he agreed to fly the goods to Managua himself. The heavily loaded plane left San Juan on December 30, and crashed into the ocean just a mile off shore. Roberto Clemente's body was never found.

Less than three months after Roberto's death, he was elected to baseball's Hall of Fame. The Baseball Writers Association, which elects the Hall of Fame's members, had voted overwhelmingly to waive the rule stating a player had to have been out of the game at least five years before becoming eligible.

In August 1973, Roberto's widow, Vera, and their sons traveled to Cooperstown, New York, to attend the ceremony. All gathered honored Roberto Clemente's greatness as both a baseball player and a humanitarian. Nearly twenty years later his name is still synonymous with the highest level of achievement.

Everett Alvarez, Jr.

Navy Pilot, Businessman

1937–

On August 4, 1964, two U.S. Navy ships radioed that they were under attack in the South China Sea, off the coast of Vietnam. North Vietnamese boats, they reported, have opened fire. The Navy sent several fighter bombers to the scene to help. When Everett Alvarez's plane found the disabled U.S. ships, the enemy boats had already left the scene.

President Lyndon B. Johnson was angry over this unprovoked attack. The United States and North Vietnam had been engaged in a war of words for many months, but until this incident, no shots had been fired. The time had come for the president to decide if he should lead his country into a full-scale war.

The next day, August 5, President Johnson ordered U.S. planes to bomb North Vietnam. Pilot Alvarez left his aircraft carrier and flew toward the small mountainous country. As he approached the coast, he spotted enemy boats and opened fire on them. The North Vietnamese fired back and hit Captain Alvarez's plane, which quickly filled with smoke.

Captain Alvarez managed to pull the ring that ejected him from the cockpit. His parachute opened, and he floated slowly down into the Gulf of Tonkin. As he neared the water, he saw Vietnamese fishermen pointing at him with high-powered rifles. After he hit the water, they pulled him into their boat, tied him up, and headed to shore. By this time the other American planes were nowhere in sight. Everett was completely alone.

Everett Alvarez, Jr., had become the first American prisoner taken during the long Vietnam War. He was not, of course, the last. During the nearly nine years that the war lasted, he would be joined in Hanoi, North Vietnam's capital, by as many as 500 POWs.

During the first year of Everett's capture, he was moved often. In one prison, rats ran across the floor all night, and cockroaches covered the vat of cold water that passed for a sink. No matter where he was, the food was barely edible, and Everett nearly starved. At first, he wondered how he would be able to survive as a prisoner of war. Gradually though, he developed the skills needed to cope. To relieve his troubled mind, he thought back on his happy childhood, trying to recapture the warmth and love of family life back in California.

Everett had spent most of his life in Salinas, where his grandparents had come from Mexico many years before as migrant farm workers. His grandmother, MaMona, had always impressed the family with her strength of mind. Survival was not taken for granted by Mexican laborers during the early twentieth century. There were always many children to feed and house and little money for anything. Everett had often been compared to his grandmother, and now he hoped he could draw on the same source of strength to get him through the difficult times ahead.

Alone in his filthy prison cell, Everett relived his high school years. He ran every track meet over and over, listening to the fans cheer him during the league championships. His parents, who'd been unable to get much education, were so proud of him when he graduated from the University of Santa Clara and then decided to become a Navy pilot. Kneeling before the cross he'd scratched into the prison wall, he prayed that his parents could find some relief from their worries about his safety.

Finally, Everett was taken to the prison in North Vietnam's capitol that became known as the Hanoi Hilton. There were other American soldiers there, and, even though they weren't allowed to speak to each other, they found various ways of communicating. By tapping codes on the cell walls the prisoners were able to give each other support.

When Ho Chi Minh, President of North Vietnam, died in September 1969, prison conditions improved a little. The food became more varied and plentiful. Most importantly, the prisoners were allowed to gather in small groups for exercise sessions. Many of the men became close friends. They all vowed to stick together and not allow the North Vietnamese to use them against each other.

Finally, in February 1973—eight and a half years after his parachute had drifted into the gulf—Everett Alvarez was released from prison. A peace agreement had been reached between the United States and North Vietnam and the war was over. Everett Alvarez flew home to California and was given a hero's welcome. In Santa Clara, 100,000 people turned out for a parade in Everett's honor.

The next several months were a whirlwind of parties and ceremonies. Everett was asked again and again to describe his years in North Vietnam. President Richard Nixon invited the POWs to a dinner at the White House. For this special occasion, Everett invited Tammy Ilyas, a woman he'd met on one of his recent trips. When the two were married in October 1973, Everett hoped to settle into a new life and finally leave the past behind.

Everett resumed his Navy career and returned to school, earning both a master's and a law degree. When he retired from the military in 1982, he was appointed by President Ronald Reagan to help run the Peace Corps. Later he was named Deputy Administrator of the Veteran's Administration in Washington, D.C.

On November 13, 1982, Everett Alvarez was asked to speak at the dedication of the Vietnam Veteran's Memorial in Washington. Carved into this black granite "V"-shaped monument are the names of the 58,000 Americans who died during the Vietnam War. Everett spoke for all veterans when he praised the courage and dedication of these men and women who, unlike himself, were not lucky enough to return home.

The dedication ceremony for the Vietnam Veteran's Memorial in Washington, D.C.

Luis Valdes

Playwright

1940–

In Luis Valdes's 1987 play, "I Don't Have to Show You No Stinking Badges," the main character, Buddy Villa, and his wife live in a comfortable home in a middle-class California community. But something's wrong. When Asians move into the neighborhood, Buddy complains that they're ruining the place. Then the Villas' son drops out of Harvard Law School to "find himself," and he criticizes his parents for leading such boring lives. The play's message? That Chicanos can be just as American as Americans, says the playwright.

Luis, the son of migrant farm workers, grew up in San Jose, California. He entered school speaking little English, but by the late 1950s, when he graduated from high school, it was his Spanish that was, he says, "in tatters." During the 1960s, however, when he joined forces with César Chávez and his farm workers' union, Luis made a point of returning to his native language and culture. He formed a theater company, El Teatro Campesino, which rode on the back of flatbed trucks performing skits for migrant farm workers. He wrote and performed only for Chicanos and urged his fellow workers to join him in celebrating their "otherness."

Gradually, though, as his talent and energy attracted attention— especially when his play "Zoot Suit" made it to the Broadway stage— Luis Valdes began to reach for a wider audience. He still wrote about Mexican Americans, but as he grew older and as both cultures changed, he began to show Chicanos in a different light. Now, it was their struggle to assimilate that interested him more.

La Bamba, the 1988 film about the short, stunning career of Ritchie Valens, portrays a young man from the *barrio*, who by virtue of raw talent and determination, becomes a rock 'n' roll star. Ritchie, a third-generation Mexican American who didn't even speak Spanish, was the ideal character for Luis Valdes. Like Luis himself, Ritchie Valens tried to be accepted by an American audience without forsaking his Chicano roots.

The film, which was one of the surprise hits of 1988, established Luis Valdes as an important American director, perhaps the *only* American who can interpret the Chicano experience for the rest of the country. It's a role Luis enjoys, but one he realizes has pitfalls, because his success threatens to take him from the very community and people that shaped his artistic vision. Like his characters, the dilemma for Luis Valdes is how to find—but not lose—yourself in America.

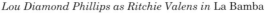

Lou Diamond Phillips as Ritchie Valens in La Bamba

Martin Sheen

Actor
1940–

In 1981, while he was in India filming the movie *Gandhi,* Martin Sheen recovered something lost since childhood—his Catholic faith. It was, he explained to an interviewer, the experience of *being* in India: ". . . you see a whole nation living on the edge of life and death . . . and yet the joy and vibrancy of life is equally impressive." The poverty Martin Sheen saw in India made him value his own life more. He enjoyed professional success, a good marriage, and a loving family. Now, he felt, the time had come to give to those who had much less.

"Martin Sheen" is the stage name of Ramon Estevez, son of a Spanish father and an Irish mother. Ramon grew up in Dayton, Ohio, but left to seek his fortune in New York City while still a senior in high school. During his first year of casting calls—when actors read scripts for television, stage, and movie producers—he decided his real name would limit him to Hispanic roles. Despite his Spanish ancestry, Ramon doesn't look Hispanic and didn't want to risk being typecast.

The young actor paid his dues—and then some—during those early, hard years in New York City. He held every imaginable job as long as it brought him in contact with theater people. Once he worked as the janitor for the off-Broadway Living Theatre. While waiting for his big break, he often ate at the Salvation Army.

Finally, the parts came. First there was television and appearances on such hit shows as "The Defenders" and "East Side, West Side." Then theater, with a supporting role in the award-winning Broadway hit, "The Subject Was Roses." In 1968, a role in the Mike Nichols' film *Catch-22* took Martin to Mexico. By then, he had a wife—Janet Templeton whom he'd married in 1961—and four children, and he was tired of trying to raise a family in Manhattan. The Sheens moved permanently to Los Angeles.

For the next twenty years, Martin Sheen appeared in such well-known movies as *Badlands*, *Apocalypse Now*, *Gandhi*, and *Wall Street*. His successful career left him little time to be with his family. When the children were young, Janet often brought them to location shoots in Central America, Europe, and the Philippines. In California, the Sheens bought a house in Malibu.

It's perhaps not surprising then that all four children were eventually bitten by the acting bug. The oldest, Emilio Estevez, began his film career soon after graduating from Santa Monica High School. His first movies, *Tex* and *The Outsiders* made in 1981 and 1982, were based on the young adult novels of S. E. Hinton. Later films included *The Breakfast Club* and *St. Elmo's Fire*. During the 1980s, Emilio also became a screenwriter.

If Emilio ever looked over his shoulder he would have seen his brother Carlos Estevez—known to movie audiences as Charlie Sheen—following closely behind. Charlie, Martin and Janet's third son, was not as good a student as Emilio and could barely wait to leave high school and get on with life. He wanted to become either a professional baseball player or an actor.

As soon as he graduated, he began visiting film producers and directors. Success followed quickly. In 1984, Charlie appeared in the movie *Red Dawn*. In 1985, he worked almost nonstop on movies such as *Ferris Bueller's Day Off* and *Lucas*. In 1986, the twenty-year-old was poised for stardom, which came in the Academy-Award–winning film, *Platoon*. In director Oliver Stone's semiautobiographical film, Charlie played the lead, a young soldier stunned by the tragedy of the Vietnam conflict. A few years later, Charlie Sheen starred in another Oliver Stone film, *Wall Street*.

Martin Sheen's two other children, son Ramon and daughter Renee, have also acted in various films. Despite the Sheen/Estevez children's successes, critics have wondered if movie parts have come too easily for Martin Sheen's children. They wonder if the fact that the Estevez kids never paid their dues has taken some of the conviction and compassion out of their work—a complaint no one ever made about Martin Sheen.

As his children discover the ins and outs of Hollywood and earn more money per film than their father earned during much of his career, Martin has turned much of his attention toward social activism. Since 1982 Martin Sheen has been arrested more than forty times for such things as trespassing at the Nevada Atomic Bomb Test Site of the atomic bomb and at various nuclear power plants around the country. A strong pacifist, he worries about the world his children's children will inherit and has vowed not to will the planet to those who would destroy it.

Voices of La Causa

Reies López Tijerina
Rodolfo "Corky" Gonzáles
José Angel Gutiérrez

Our father, the Spaniard, left us. We decided to stay with our mother, the Indian, here in New Mexico. . . . We were born as the consequences of a conflict of races and cultures, when the Spanish discovered, explored, and Christianized this continent. Out of that conflict came a New Breed, a new people. Sometimes we are known as La Raza, which is the Race, the People. But the name we are known by does not matter. We are a New Breed.[23]

—Reies López Tijerina

La Raza expresses the pride Mexican Americans feel in their rich cultural heritage. The term says to other Americans, and particularly to the Anglo community, "We are not ashamed of our mixed blood, our brown skin, our Spanish language. We are unique."

La Raza is a term borrowed from the countries of Latin America, where it implies a new family of man. This new race includes the area's original inhabitants, the Indians, plus all others who've come since Columbus's first voyage five hundred years ago. Interestingly, south of the Rio Grande, October 12 is celebrated not as Columbus Day but as "el Dia de la Raza."

Mexican-American pride makes the injustices suffered in the United States hard to bear. Prejudice and discrimination, they know, have taken their toll on many generations. The Chicano desire to right the wrongs of the past and assure a bright future for all has lead to the formation of a movement called La Causa—"the Cause."

One leader of La Causa, César Chávez, made nonviolence his main principle. Others have believed gains could only be made with the threat—either subtle or outright—of violence. The leaders of the movement are as varied as the tactics. From Henry B. Gonzáles to César Chávez to Corky Gonzáles, Reies López Tijerina, and José Angel Gutiérrez, the message was always the same—together we can make a difference.

During the 1960s and 1970s, the voices of the following men rose to call their people to action.

Reies López Tijerina

Reies Tijerina's name translates loosely to "King of the Tigers," and these words well describe this Chicano leader's flare for drama and cunning. Born in a Texas cotton field, this evangelist minister is best known for reviving the land-grant question in New Mexico and for trying to claim millions of acres of lands illegally seized since the 1848 Treaty of Guadalupe Hidalgo.

In 1966, Reies Tijerina was jailed following an attempt by his group, the *Alianza Federal de Mercedes* (Federal Alliance of Land Grants), to seize part of New Mexico's Kit Carson National Forest. In the following letter, he addresses the issues of great importance to the Alianza.

A Letter from Jail

From my cell block in this jail I am writing these reflections. I write them to my people, the Indo-Hispanos, to my friends among the Anglos, to the agents of the federal government, the state of New Mexico, the Southwest, and the entire Indo-Hispano world—"Latin America."

. . . What is my real crime? As I and the poor people see it, especially the Indo-Hispano, my only crime is UPHOLDING OUR RIGHTS AS PROTECTED BY THE TREATY OF GUADALUPE HIDALGO,

which ended the so-called Mexican American war of 1846–48. . . .
Ever since the treaty was signed in 1848, our people have been asking
every elected President of the United States for a redress of grievances.
. . . Our right to the Spanish land-grant pueblos is the real reason
why I am in prison at this moment.

The Indo-Hispano world will never trust the United States as long
as this government occupies our land illegally. The honest policy of
the United States will have to begin at home. . . . Our property,
freedom, and culture must be respected in New Mexico, in the whole
Southwest, before the Anglo can expect to be trusted in South America,
Mexico, and Canada. . . .

. . . While others are free, building their personal empires, I am
in jail for defending and fighting for the rights of my people. Only
my Indo-Hispano people have influenced me to be what I am. I am
what I am, for my brothers.[24]

Rodolfo Corky Gonzáles

Like many other Mexican-Americans, Corky Gonzáles understands
the problems of the poor from first-hand experience. He was born
in the barrio of Denver, Colorado, and worked in that state's sugar-
beet fields. To escape a life of constant poverty, he trained as a
prize fighter. Later, however, he became a businessman and government official and, in the mid-1960s, a spokesman for Chicano
youth.

Corky Gonzáles came to believe that the only way for Mexican
Americans to feel pride in their heritage was to rediscover their
common origin. In the following excerpt from "The Spiritual Plan
of Aztlán," he presses his fellow members of La Raza to seek out
Aztlán, the home of the Aztec Indians in the Southwestern United
States.

In the spirit of a new people that is conscious not only of its proud
historical heritage but also of the brutal "gringo" [Anglo] invasion

of our territories, we, the Chicano inhabitants and civilizers of the northern land of Aztlán, whenever came our forefathers, reclaiming the land of their birth and consecrating the determination of our people of the sun, declare the call of our blood is our power, our responsibility, and our inevitable destiny. . . .

Aztlán belongs to those who plant the seeds, water the fields, and gather the crops, and not to the foreign Europeans. . .

Brotherhood unites us, and love for our brothers makes us a people whose time has come and who struggles against the foreigner. . . . With our heart in our hands and our hands in the soil, we declare the independence of our Mestizo Nation. We are a bronze people with a bronze culture. Before the world, before all of North America, before all our brothers on the Bronze Continent, we are a nation, we are a union of free pueblos, we are Aztlán.[25]

José A. Gutiérrez (left) and Rodolfo "Corky" González (right) at Raza Unida Party National Convention in 1972

José Angel Gutiérrez

In 1968, when José Gutiérrez wrote "22 Miles," he was a college student and had already helped found both MAYO (Mexican-American Youth Organization) and La Raza Unida, which became La Raza's main political arm. In 1970, La Raza Unida successfully backed two candidates for election to the school board in Crystal City, Texas. The candidates won, and, for the first time, Crystal City had a Mexican-American school board majority. The election has since come to symbolize the importance of strength through unity.

In this autobiographical poem, which harkens back to the farcical Mexican *vacilada* songs, Gutiérrez describes how, over the course of twenty-two miles, or years, he's come to think of his Mexican heritage.

From 22 I see my first 8 weren't.
Around the 9th I was called "meskin."
By the 10th, I knew and believed I was.
I found out what it meant to know, to believe . . .
    before my 13th.
Through brown eyes, seeing only brown colors and feeling
only brown feelings . . . I saw . . . I felt . . . I hated. . .
I cried . . . I tried . . . I didn't understand during these 4.
I rested by just giving up.
While, on the side . . . I realized I BELIEVED in
white as pretty,
my being governor,
blond blue-eyed baby Jesus,
cokes and hamburgers,
equality for all regardless of race, creed, or color,
Mr. Williams our banker.
I had to!
That was all I had.
At the 19th mile, I fought blindly at everything and
    anything.

Not knowing, Not caring about WHY, WHEN, or FOR WHAT.
I fought.   And fought.
By the 21st, I was tired and tried.
       But now. . . .
I've been told that I am dangerous.
That is because I am good at not being a Mexican
That is because I know now that I have been cheated.
That is because I hate circumstances and love choices.
You know . . . chorizo tacos y tortillas ARE good,
   even at school. . . .
At 22, my problems are still the same but now I know I am
                    your problem.
That farm boys, Mexican and Negro boys are in Vietnam is
            but one thing I think about:
      Crystal City, Texas 78839
      The migrant worker;
      The good gringo:
Staying Mexican enough;
Helping;
Looking at the world from the back of a truck. . . . .[26]

Part Five

Looking Toward the Twenty-First Century:
A Wider Audience

By the year 2000, there may well be more than 31 million Hispanic Americans, making them the largest minority in the United States. Yet will they be able to translate their strength in numbers into political, economic, and cultural power? The answer is a hopeful "yes," if the examples of those men and women whose stories are told in this section serve as guides.

Of course, as always, it's the diversity of the Hispanic population that is both its strength and weakness. And by the start of the twenty-first century, their differences may be even more startling. From inner-city New York Puerto Ricans to wealthy Cubans in Miami to farm workers from the fertile valleys of California to political refugees from Nicaragua, El Salvador, and Honduras—the range of interests and needs will be difficult to comprehend.

Perhaps, as people such as Oscar Hijuelos, Ellen Ochoa, Luis Valdes, Antonia Novello, and Evelyn Cisneros—to name only a few—can show, the focus of twenty-first century Hispanic America should not be on "strengths" or "weaknesses" but instead on "richness." America, it seems, hungers for things Hispanic—music, art, dance, literature, food, design. With increased political participation, this huge ethnic group will have the nation's attention for once and for all. From then on, Hispanics may no longer have to, as Henry Cisneros once said, "look at a decade and say 'Where did it go?'"

Joan Baez

Singer
1941–

Amazing grace, how sweet the sound
That saved a wretch like me.
I once was lost, but now I'm found.
Was blind, but now I see.

Joan Baez chose this old black spiritual to open the historic Live Aid concert in 1985. Most people in the crowd of 90,000 at Philadelphia's JFK Stadium hadn't even been born when Joan launched her career in 1960. Yet Joan knew from long expcrience that the message of this song would reach out to everyone in the audience, no matter what age. When she spoke to the rock music fans she asked them to join her in saying "grace." Her strong, pure voice brought the noisy crowd to a hush.

Twenty years before Joan Baez's music had seized the attention of an entire generation. They listened to her lovely soprano sing "Blowing in the Wind" and "We Shall Overcome," and they joined the Queen of Folk Music in trying to change the world.

When eighteen-year-old Joan Baez burst onto the folk music scene, she was just leaving the security of a close, loving family. Her father, Dr. Alberto Vicio Baez, was a physicist who'd come to the United States from Puebla, Mexico, when he was only two. Joan's mother, Joan Brook, was still an infant when her parents moved to New York from Edinburgh, Scotland.

Joan Brook met Alberto Baez at a dance in New York City. The singer's mother recalls that she couldn't help but notice the handsome Latin as he stood making airplane noises in the midst of a crowd of admiring women. He looked over at Joan and winked and she looked away. From this first meeting, love blossomed and the two were married a year later.

During the next seven years, three daughters were born to the couple: Pauline, Joan, and Mimi. During the mid-1940s, Alberto decided to attend graduate school in mathematics at Stanford University, and the family moved to California. Later, they moved back to New York State—this time to Cornell University—for a time while Alberto worked as a research physicist. In the early 1950s, Alberto took a job with the United Nations, and the family moved to Iraq, a country that captured young Joan's imagination.

In 1958, Professor Alberto Baez began teaching at the Massachusetts Institute of Technology, and the family moved to the Boston area. At the time coffeehouses were all the rage at Cambridge's Harvard Square, and one evening Dr. Baez took Joan with him to hear some of the popular young folksingers. Joan was immediately taken by the folk music scene. From then on, she spent as much time as possible playing her own guitar and learning traditional folk ballads. Soon she, too, was performing in Cambridge's coffeehouses.

Joan soon caught the attention of a music promoter. He booked her into a Chicago club, the Gate of Horn, where she played for two weeks. There she met a singer named Bob Gibson, who invited her to appear with him that summer—1959—at the Newport, Rhode Island, Folk Festival. She sang two songs with Gibson making a deep impression on the audience of 13,000.

The next year she appeared again in Newport. This time her solo appearance was followed by several offers from record companies to produce her first album. She chose a small label, Vanguard, and during the fall of 1960 spent several weeks at a recording studio in New York City. By Christmas, the album, *Joan Baez*, was on sale around the country.

After recording the album, Joan first returned to Boston, and then she and her boyfriend decided to move to California. They packed up a rickety Corvair with everything they owned and headed West. When, several weeks later, they arrived in San Francisco, they were greeted with the news that Joan's album, which she'd scarcely thought about during the long drive, was selling very well. In fact, it was soon declared a major hit. Joan's star was definitely rising. In fact, her life would never be the same again.

The success of her first record was followed by almost constant touring. As that first wild year of success closed, she visited a folk club in New York City, where she saw for the first time a scruffy young singer who looked like an "urban hillbilly." She asked to be introduced to the singer, Bob Dylan, and for years afterward the two names were linked both privately and professionally.

By 1963, Joan had recorded her third album and was appearing before crowds of 20,000 people. Her political activism was growing but it wasn't yet considered outside of the American mainstream. She'd even been asked to sing at a gala for President John F. Kennedy. When Kennedy was assassinated and Lyndon Baines Johnson became president, the gala went ahead as scheduled. Joan shocked the assembled Washington dignitaries with one of Bob Dylan's songs: "The Times They Are A-Changing."

During the 1960s, Joan's aching songs seemed right in synch with the turmoil felt by America's young people. The civil rights movement and the Vietnam War left Americans of various backgrounds feeling angry and frustrated. Joan's music seemed to help these disillusioned Americans sort out their feelings about peace and war and injustice.

Throughout a career that has spanned thirty years—and continues strong today—Joan Baez has recorded albums of different styles, bringing something new to country and western, rock, and international folk music. In 1974, her album *Gracias a la Vida*, sung entirely in Spanish, featured songs of love and death from Central and South America. She dedicated the album to her father, Alberto Baez, who, she wrote, "gave me my Latin name and whatever optimism about life I may claim to have."

*Rev. Martin Luther King, Jr., leads a group of people
that included Joan Baez in 1966. The group
escorted black children to their newly integrated school.*

Los Angeles's Pachucos and the Zoot Suit Riots of 1942

Two cultures clashed on the streets of Los Angeles in June 1943, and neither was ever the same again. On one side of the schism were the *Pachucos*, gang members from the city's Mexican-American community. These young men had already grabbed attention with their zoot suits—high-waisted baggy pants and long suit coats with very broad shoulders—which all but screamed "I am different!" to Los Angeles's uneasy Anglo community. On the other side, were U.S. Navy sailors, waiting restlessly to be shipped out for war service in the Pacific.

Los Angeles had been tense since the summer before, when a Chicano boy was found murdered in an area known as the Sleepy Lagoon. Police decided the killer had to be from one of the many Mexican street gangs, and they promptly went to the city's eastside community and arrested twenty-three Mexican-American boys. During the trial, several witnesses for the prosecution made shockingly racist statements. When twelve gang members were found guilty of murder in January 1943, many in the community felt the boys's only crime was that they were Mexican.

The pachuco gang members, who became the infamous zoot suiters, were the children of migrant workers who'd crossed the U.S.–Mexican border during the 1920s to do farm and railroad work. These immigrants, fleeing desperate poverty in Mexico, were happy for any job. By the 1940s, however, their children, many who were born in the United States and therefore were American citizens, had grown dissatisfied with bad housing, bad schools, and bad jobs.

These young Mexican Americans were stung, too, by the anti-Mexican prejudice they felt from the Anglo community. They wanted a way to express their feelings of frustration and bitterness, and they found it in their outrageous clothes and hairstyles.

The Los Angeles police, however, didn't see the zoot suiters as just more rebellious teenagers. The Pachucos, they believed, were a threat to public order. The sailors and other military men on leave in Los Angeles viewed these wildly dressed Mexicans as un-American and therefore good targets. These servicemen were, as one of them later testified, itching to fight.

Zoot suiters being detained by Los Angeles Police.

Tensions rose throughout May 1943. There were small clashes here and there. Then, during the first hot days of June, sailors began roaming the streets of Los Angeles, pulling zoot suiters off buses and out of houses and beating them up. Many had their clothes ripped off and their hair cut. By June 7, the "tension" had turned into an undeclared war on Mexican Americans. Cars full of sailors drove up and down the streets looking for zoot suiters. The police stood by and watched.

It was just a matter of time before the Mexican community boiled over in the face of this unjust attack. Spanish-language newspapers asked for calm; English papers seem to egg on the military attackers. What began as street fights, turned into a major race riot—

Zoot Suiters

". . . the ugliest brand of mob action since the coolie [Chinese] race riots of the 1870s," wrote *Time* magazine that summer. Rioting soon spread to Pasadena, Long Beach, and San Diego. The national press began to report the story and soon riots also broke out in such eastern cities as Chicago, Detroit, and Philadelphia.

The riots continued until the Mexican ambassador in Washington asked the U.S. State Department to help stop the violence. Embarrassed government officials began investigating and found that sailors had indeed attacked unarmed citizens and that neither the Los Angeles police nor military officials had done anything to stop them. They ordered that all military leaves be canceled and servicemen be kept close to their barracks. The rioting soon stopped.

When tempers had cooled a bit, both the Mexican and Anglo communities began looking at the causes of what became known as the Zoot-Suit Riots. Conferences and hearings were held and many from both sides began looking hard at the frustrations felt by young Mexican Americans. Many agreed that since the children of migrant workers were now U.S. citizens, they needed to be encouraged to take part in American life. The way to accomplish this, officials agreed, was through better education and job training. Agreeing on the causes of the rioting, however, would turn out to be the easy part. *Solving* the problems created by years of prejudice would be another matter altogether.

Ritchie Valens

Singer, Songwriter

1942–1959

When Richard Valenzuela stepped up to the microphone at the American Legion hall that night in 1957, everyone knew they were in the presence of a star. He wasn't quite seventeen years old, yet he carried himself as though he'd been a rock musician for a decade. Maybe, in a way, he had been—for as long as he could remember, all he'd thought about was playing his guitar, singing his songs, and making people dance.

Richard's electric guitar was his lifeline to the world outside the *barrio*. Sometimes at night in his bed, he would reach out and touch the guitar's steel frame, just to make sure it was still there. Without his guitar, he might be doomed to a life, like his parents', of picking fruit and living in migrant labor camps. Or worse, he might end up like his older half-brother, a troubled, small-time crook.

So, when he had his chance to perform in public, he sang and played as though his life depended on it. And for the next year, everything that could go right did. First, a small-label record producer decided to take a chance on him, and the first Ritchie Valens—the name was created by the producer—single, "Come on Let's Go," shot up the pop charts so fast the Valenzuelas could barely catch their breaths.

The next thing Ritchie knew, teenagers all over Los Angeles and Southern California flocked to hear him and then beg for his autograph. When his girlfriend's father would not allow his daughter to date the rising star, he wrote the song "Donna" for her and that, too, became a hit.

Then came the tours. Ritchie traveled all over the United States with various rock-and-roll stars—Jackie Wilson, Eddie Cochrane, Buddy Holly, among others. He appeared on Dick Clark's "American Bandstand" and sang in huge halls in New York City and Chicago. Back home in L.A., he drove the boulevards in his shiny new car and bought his mother a suburban ranch house.

In January 1959, Ritchie's rock version of the traditional Mexican folk song "La Bamba" became his third smash hit in a row. Ritchie sang the song in Spanish, the language of his grandfathers, but which he himself didn't speak. "La Bamba" is still Ritchie's best-known song—the one that will always be linked with his name.

Then, on February 4, 1959, Ritchie Valens's music stopped. On a stormy, snowy night after a concert in Clear Lake, Iowa, Ritchie, Buddy Holly, and a singer called the Big Bopper, boarded a charter plane for Fargo, North Dakota. The plane crashed into an Iowa cornfield, and three of America's best-known stars were killed. Ritchie Valens was only seventeen.

Two more records were released after Ritchie's death: "That's My Little Susie" in March 1959 and "Little Girl" in July 1959. In 1988, a movie of Ritchie's life, "La Bamba" directed by Luis Valdes, was released and became a huge hit. Thirty years after the songs were written, a new generation of rock music lovers discovered the music of Ritchie Valens.

Antonia Coelho Novello

U.S. Surgeon General

1944–

The report said that fewer Hispanic Americans have health insurance than any other ethnic group. Hispanics have higher rates of diabetes, high blood pressure, and certain kinds of cancer. To make matters worse, they are also being hit hard by AIDS. These findings appeared in a special issue of the *Journal of the American Medical Association* in 1990. And even though the head of the study team, Dr. Antonia C. Novello, had recently been made the U.S. surgeon general—the nation's chief doctor—the report also complained that there were too few Hispanics in the health professions.

Antonia C. Novello bucked all the odds to become the first Hispanic *and* the first female surgeon general. She's not, however, one to spend much time looking around to see who's watching her. She's been a dedicated student of science and medicine since she can remember, and the rest has simply followed from that.

Born in Fajardo, Puerto Rico, Antonia Coelho received her bachelor of science degree in 1965 from the University of Puerto Rico. She then traveled north to Baltimore to attend graduate school in public health at the Johns Hopkins University. After receiving her master's degree, she returned to medical school at the University of Puerto Rico. She later specialized in pediatrics at the University of Michigan and Georgetown University.

Known for her compassion and energy, she rose to deputy director of the National Institute of Child Health and Human Development before being tapped for the surgeon general's post. As a pediatrician, she is especially concerned with how such things as the AIDS epidemic and a lack of adequate health care affect the youngest members of society.

Since being sworn into her post in March 1990, she has made headlines with sharp attacks on both smoking and the tobacco industry and with her report on the health of Hispanic Americans. In her introduction to the AMA report, Dr. Novello urged that the United States find ways to help those Hispanics most in need. The group is so diverse, she said, that often health care workers and government officials are insensitive to the special needs of people who are lumped together as "Hispanics." Cuban Americans in Miami, for example, have different problems from Mexican Americans living along the Rio Grande. She hopes the study itself might lead the fight against inadequate Hispanic health care. Dr. Novello would also be pleased if her own example showed other Hispanics the rewards of a career in medicine.

Henry Cisneros
Elected Official
1947–

The first time Henry Cisneros ran for a seat on San Antonio's city council, hardly anyone thought he had a chance of winning. Neither conservatives nor liberals felt he was really *their* candidate. Many in the Mexican-American community of this large south Texas city thought he was too cozy with the Anglos, or whites, in the business community. The Anglos, for their part, had never even considered voting for a Hispanic. What would happen to 'ol San Antone, they wondered, if a man named Cisneros held a council seat?

To make matters worse, Henry Cisneros had almost no money for campaign expenses. But he was so determined to win the election, he decided to run literally for the seat—and run hard. Candidate Cisneros in running shoes became a common sight on the streets of San Antonio. He attended every block party or picnic or barbecue he could get himself invited to. He sent out his own daily press releases and made sure he was mentioned frequently in newspapers and on television. When Election Day 1975 was over, Henry Cisneros had won the right to become the youngest member ever to serve on the city council of San Antonio.

In many ways, everything in Henry's life had led him to this very point. Born in San Antonio in 1947, Henry's father, George Cisneros, had spent his boyhood as a migrant worker in Colorado.

He saw firsthand the devastating effects of poverty on Mexican-American laborers and vowed he would break the cycle in his own family. George became the first Cisneros to graduate from high school. He then attended business school and when World War II broke out he joined the army, eventually rising to the rank of colonel. Education and discipline were the two qualities he wanted most to pass on to his own five children.

Kindergarten was a confusing experience for Henry Cisneros since, for the first time in his life, he was expected to speak only in English. Spanish, after all, was the language of both the Cisneros household and their San Antonio neighborhood. But Henry learned his second language quickly. During high school, at least one teacher had noticed Henry's "genius for the spoken word and his ability to sway people with it."

After high school, Henry entered Texas A & M University. He wanted to become, he thought, an army officer just like his father. By the time he graduated in 1968, he had become interested in a new field called urban planning, which looked at the way cities grow and change. After earning a master's degree from Texas A & M, Henry and his new wife, Mary Alice, moved to Washington, D.C., so that Henry could study for his doctoral degree at George Washington University.

Henry not only completed his Ph.D., but in 1973, he earned a second master's degree in public administration from Harvard University. His young family—his daughter Teresa was born in 1971—had had enough, however. It was, they decided, time to go home.

When they returned to San Antonio in 1974 the city was beginning to change quickly. Its population was growing, and the city's ability to provide services was stretched. New leadership was needed. Henry decided to put his education to practical use on the city council, where he served for six years.

By 1981, Henry Cisneros believed he was ready to lead the city as mayor. Again, voters were impressed by the young candidate's personality and energy. Henry's eloquence was noticed by the national press, too, and much attention was focused on San Antonio. When Election Day 1981 was over, Henry Cisneros had won almost 62 percent of the vote.

Mayor Cisneros had some big ideas for San Antonio—the kinds of ideas he'd been dreaming about since he was a graduate student. He wanted to encourage tourists and convention-goers to visit the Alamo City. He felt, too, that communication and computer industries were the right ones for south Texas and set out to bring high-tech firms to the Austin–San Antonio corridor.

Both Mayor Cisneros and his policies were very popular. When Henry ran for a second term in 1983, he captured more than 94.25 percent of the vote. Soon the national spotlight was on him once again. In 1984, the Democratic Party's nominee for President, Walter Mondale, named Mayor Cisneros to his list of candidates for the vice-presidential slot. Henry and his family met with the Mondales and with the national press. Henry wasn't chosen but many were impressed with this bright, young Hispanic American. Henry's star was clearly rising.

Then, in 1987, Henry and Mary Alice's third child and first son was born and all their plans changed. John Paul Anthony Cisneros was born with severe health problems, including a defective heart. The Cisneros family now needed Henry more than ever, and the mayor decided to put his political career on hold.

Mayor Henry Cisneros brought new energy and vision to San Antonio. His command of the issues, his appeal to both Hispanic and Anglo voters, and his eloquence have attracted attention from across the country. Many believe he is the most likely of all current Hispanic political leaders to move into the national arena. "There is still much to be done," Henry said recently. And many are waiting to see just how much.

Henry Cisneros and family

Richard Rodriquez

Writer, Teacher

1948–

One morning in the early 1950s, a Mexican-American boy entered the first grade at a neighborhood Roman Catholic elementary school in Sacramento, California. "Boys and girls," he heard the nun say. "This is *Rich-heard Road-ree-guess.*"

The boy had never heard his name in English, and he was stunned. He turned to look at his mother, who'd been standing in the doorway as her son entered the classroom. She turned to leave, and Richard felt his childhood departing with her.

Some thirty years later, in his autobiography *Hunger of Memory: The Education of Richard Rodriquez*, the former Catholic schoolboy, now professor and author, describes how this early school experience shaped his ideas about education and, specifically, about bilingual education. How would his life have been different, he asks, if he'd attended a school where Spanish was spoken? His early years might have been happier and more secure, but his entire education would have suffered. When a child goes to school, Rodriquez argues, he must leave his family's world behind. School is "public," and family is "private." Spanish was his private language—the language he used at home—and English was public. The great lesson of school, he writes, is to gain a *public* identity.

At first his English was very bad:

> I was unable to hear my own sounds, but I knew very well that I
> spoke English poorly. My words could not stretch far enough to form
> complete thoughts. And the words I did speak I didn't know well
> enough to make into distinct sounds. (Listeners would usually lower
> their heads, better to hear what I was trying to say.) But it was one
> thing for me to speak English with difficulty. It was more troubling
> for me to hear my parents speak in public; their high-whining vowels
> and guttural consonants; their sentences that got stuck with 'eh' and
> 'ah' sounds; the confused syntax; the hesitant rhythm of sounds so
> different from the way gringos spoke. I'd notice, moreover, that my
> parents' voices were softer than those of gringos we'd meet.

> . . . There were many times like the night at a brightly lit gasoline
> station . . . when I stood uneasily, hearing my father. He was talking
> to a teenaged attendant. I do not recall what they were saying, but
> I cannot forget the sounds my father made as he spoke. At one point
> his words slid together to form one word—sounds as confused as the
> threads of blue and green oil in the puddle next to my shoes. His
> voice rushed through what he had left to say. . . . I looked away
> to the lights of passing automobiles. I tried not to hear anymore. But
> I heard only too well the calm, easy tones in the attendant's reply.
> Shortly afterward, walking toward home with my father, I shivered
> when he put his hand on my shoulder. The very first chance that
> I got, I evaded his grasp and ran on ahead into the dark. . . .[27]

School was often a painful experience for Richard Rodriquez. He
would undoubtedly have felt much less afraid had his elementary
schoolteachers spoken Spanish in the classroom. He could have raised
his hand, and his voice, and not worried about his classmates
snickering at his accent or grammar. But childhood always carries
some pain. And that pain is necessary, he writes, to acquire the
education needed to prosper in the larger world.

Richard Rodriquez became a very successful student. He graduated from Stanford University and went on to graduate school at

Columbia University in New York City and University of California at Berkeley, where he received his Ph.D. in English. He taught at Berkeley for a time but decided that instead of becoming a full-time college professor, he would spend his life reading and writing.

Today Richard Rodriquez writes about Hispanic Americans and the issues of importance to them. As with the subject of bilingual education, he doesn't always take the popular or "correct" view. His own experience—and education—have taught him that easy solutions are no match for difficult challenges.

Hunger of Memory

THE EDUCATION OF
RICHARD RODRIGUEZ

An Autobiography

Rubén Blades

Singer, Composer, Actor

1948–

I n the 1985 film *Crossover Dreams*, Rubén Blades plays a New York salsa singer named Rudy Veloz. Tired of working for next to nothing in small Latino nightclubs, Rudy decides to do whatever is necessary to cross over— that is, to perform the songs that appeal to both Hispanic and Anglo audiences. Rudy's first crossover record is a failure, however, and he feels cast adrift in the big world. His new Anglo "friends" aren't interested in him anymore; his Hispanic friends feel betrayed, and they, too, turn away. Rudy's crossover dream becomes a crossover nightmare.

The hazards of crossing over are all too familiar to Rubén Blades, who was already an international star when he released his first album in English. Featured on that 1988 album, *Nothing But the Truth*, are many of the best-known names in British and American rock––Elvis Costello, Sting, and Lou Reed. Yet even though some critics called the record "perfect," it didn't attract the mainstream American rock fans and, as was probably to be expected, the music was largely ignored by Hispanics.

In many ways, Rubén Blades is the perfect person to cross over— or as he prefers to call it "to meet halfway." Born in Panama City, Panama, he taught himself to sing and play guitar by listening to the radio. At first, he listened only to American music, especially the rock and roll and doo-wop so popular during the 1950s. After 1964, however, when during a student-led demonstration, U.S. troops opened fire on Panamanian civilians and killed twenty-one, Rubén Blades rejected American culture and for many years would not sing in English.

He enrolled in the law school of the University of Panama and in his spare time played and sang with an Afro-Cuban band. During one school vacation, he traveled to New York and made his first album, *De Panamá a Nueva York*. Then he went back to his studies in Panama, where he obtained a law degree.

In 1974, Rubén Blades returned to New York and began recording for a salsa label, Fania Records. He toured with a band called the Fania All-Stars and gradually emerged as an appealing, articulate singer and songwriter. Some referred to him as the Latino Bob Dylan.

By the early 1980s, Rubén was ready for a solo career. He wanted to move beyond salsa and create what he referred to as the Caribbean combo sound that he remembered hearing in Panama. He organized a band called Seis del Solar (Tenement Six). In 1984, Rubén signed a contract with Elektra/Asylum Records and recorded *Buscando América* (Searching for America). The album's seven songs used Latin and Caribbean rhythms, combined with jazz, soul, rock, and reggae, to tell stark, somber stories of life in Latin America. The record was a solid hit and made *Time* magazine's list of the ten best rock albums of the year.

Despite the success of *Buscando América*, Rubén decided to take a break from recording during 1984–85 and go back to school. He enrolled at Harvard University and in 1985 received his master's degree in international law.

Back in New York City, Rubén continued performing, including an appearance at Carnegie Hall. He recorded another album,

Escensas, which includes a song "Silencios," in which he sings a duet with Linda Ronstadt. The songs move away from political commentary and, instead, concentrate on themes of romance, personal relationships, and grieving.

In some ways, *Nothing But the Truth* —recorded just before Rubén's fortieth birthday—takes the singer back to his early days in Panama City when he sang and played guitar with the radio. In this album, he says, "I wanted to present a whole fabric of different colors and sounds and put them together on a record the way I remembered radio to be when radio played all different kinds of music."

Rubén Blades looks toward a bright future of music, films, and, perhaps, a return to Panama and a leap into politics. With his broad education, he feels a political role in the "new" Panama may be inevitable. He would bring the same courage and conviction to public life that he's brought to the world of popular music.

Rubén Blades in the motion picture Milagro Bean Fields

Oscar Hijuelos

Novelist

1948–

When, during the 1950s, revolution came to Cuba, Pedro Tellerina left Havana and moved to Miami. The distance between the two cities is only one hundred miles or so, but it might as well have been a million for the change it made in Pedro's life. In Havana, Pedro had played the string bass in Xavier Cugat's band in Miami he worked construction. Nothing was left of the old life, just the photos of him and his friends playing mambo music in such Havana nightclubs as the Tropicana. Pedro taped these well-worn pictures to the walls of his garage in Miami. When Pedro's young nephew, Oscar Hijuelos, would visit from New York City, he would show them to Oscar. The two would look at the black-and-white images, and Pedro would tell his nephew what it was like playing mambo music with guys such as Cugie and Desi Arnaz.

Oscar Hijuelos never forgot his uncle's stories of a time in Cuba when music seemed more important than politics. In his second novel, *The Mambo Kings Play Songs of Love*, he tells about two Cuban musicians who arrive in New York City during the 1950s and try desperately to appear on the "I Love Lucy" TV show. In 1989, this sad and funny story and its thirty-eight-year-old author won the Pulitzer Prize for Literature.

Oscar Hijuelos was born in New York City and has spent nearly all his life in Spanish Harlem. His own parents came from Cuba during the 1940s seeking not political asylum but opportunity, something they couldn't find under the harsh dictatorship of Fulgencio Batista y Zaldívar.

Spanish was Oscar's first language and he might have remained a stranger in English had it not been for a childhood illness that landed him in a Connecticut hospital for a year. As Oscar remembers, "I went in speaking Spanish and came out speaking English."

Of his childhood among the Cubans of Spanish Harlem, he remembers the endless talk about the old life in Havana, which in the memories of his family and friends became a mythic place. Many Cubans were especially interested in the success of their countryman, Desi Arnaz. Oscar's father, who cared nothing about television, never missed an episode of "I Love Lucy." His son remembers everyone in the family gathering around the television set, waiting for the familiar rumba music in the theme song to begin.

After graduating from high school, Oscar Hijuelos drifted from job to job, at one point even becoming a farmer in Wisconsin. When he returned to New York City, he enrolled in college and decided to try his hand at writing. His first novel, *Our House in the Lost World*, was published in 1983, and received wide praise. Critics found Oscar's style unusual—more Latin, they said, than American. Oscar's first novel won him the Rome Prize for Literature, and he set off to claim his winnings—one year, all expenses paid in Rome—with a suitcase full of old newspaper clippings about Cuban mambo musicians. He was ready to start his second novel.

Now that *The Mambo Kings Play Songs of Love* has made Oscar Hijuelos a literary star, he faces the challenge of bringing back to his life the calm and quiet needed to write. Creating a successful third novel might be his greatest challenge. *Mambo Kings* will soon be a motion picture, and in Oscar's Spanish Harlem apartment, the phone never seems to stop ringing. Often it's a Latin musician or out-of-work actor, wanting to know if the famous Señor Hijuelos can help with a break into the big time.

The Xavier Cugat Orchestra

Lena Guerrero

Chairman, Texas Railroad Commission

1957–

Oil is king in Texas, and, in 1991, Lena Guerrero found herself regulating the kingdom. Appointed by Governor Ann Richards to serve the remaining two years of a six-year term on the Texas Railroad Commission, Lena took over the chairmanship in April 1991. The commission, which regulates oil, gas, and transportation's interests in Texas, is one of the state's most important agencies.

At first glance, it might seem an unlikely job for the fifth of eleven children of a Mexican-American family from Mission, Texas. Lena's father, who had prospered as the manager of a local lumberyard, died of cancer when Lena was eleven. Her mother, who had never worked outside the home, took a job in a local school cafeteria. To make ends meet, the Guerrero children all took part-time jobs, many doing migrant farm work in west Texas.

Lena continued working part-time after she entered the University of Texas at Austin. She also became active in campus politics in Austin and then, after graduation, served on the city council. In 1981, at the age of twenty-six, she ran for a seat in the Texas House of Representatives and won the first of four terms, serving a district that includes downtown Austin. In 1990, *Texas Monthly* called her one of the state's ten best legislators. Lena was in the midst of her fourth term in the House when newly elected Governor Richards tapped her for a seat on the Railroad Commission.

To be sure, her appointment to the commission has been somewhat controversial. Oil and gas companies gasped at the thought of a liberal environmentalist becoming chair of the commission that oversees such things as drilling rights and land-use permits. She is, in effect, the state's secretary of energy. But Lena looks forward to setting the fears of business interests to rest. She hopes to show that she is the hard-working, open-minded public servant oil and gas concerns need in Austin. Lena will face tough opposition in the 1992 election for her seat on the commission, but she looks confidently toward the future. Lena Guerrero's rising political star is being watched closely by many voters—Hispanic and otherwise—throughout Texas and the rest of the country.

The Texas State Capitol Building in Austin

Cuba's Miami

1959

After the Spanish-American War of 1898, the United States cast a long shadow over Cuba. The island nation *was* free, but its huge northern neighbor wanted to make sure it remained safe and "helpful." The Platt Amendment of 1901, which gave the United States the right to install military bases and mobilize troops whenever they thought Cuba was in trouble, assured that, in reality, Cuba was anything but free.

American companies moved into Cuba quickly, making huge investments and virtually taking control of the country's economy. Americans were happy when in 1933 a dictator, Fulgencio Batista y Zaldívar (called Batista), took over and gave them everything they wanted. Batista's rule also assured that the living conditions of Cuban workers were only slightly better than when the Spanish governed—which, of course, meant they were miserable.

In the late 1940s, a young lawyer named Fidel Castro became the leader of Cuba's main opposition party. In 1956, Castro began a guerrilla war against the Batista regime, using the Sierra Maestra Mountains as his group's base. Three years later, Batista was deposed and Castro took control of the Cuban government.

Just as many American businessmen feared, one of Castro's first acts was to seize control of Cuba's resources—land, industry, and commerce—from U.S.-owned companies. All private property was eventually taken by the government and, not surprisingly, those who'd owned most of it left the country. Many members of the well-educated upper and middle classes headed for Miami, Florida, a little more than 100 miles from Havana.

Miami welcomed the early Cuban refugees with open arms. At the time—1959—Miami was in decline. Many of its former residents and businesses had fled to the suburbs. An influx of ambitious, well-educated Cubans—engineers, lawyers, doctors, accountants, teachers—was just what Florida's largest city needed. Miami helped its new citizens with money and tax relief so they could settle in and restart their lives.

And the Cubans repaid their new hometown for its hospitality. They started new businesses and brought the once-crumbling city back to life. Before long, Cuban Americans in Miami had higher average incomes than non-Hispanic whites. They held one-third of all banking jobs and controlled half the city's construction businesses. Altogether, Cuban Americans were responsible for 18,000 new

Cuban immigrants arriving in Miami.

businesses, many of them small and family-run. What's more, the numerous Cuban business ventures brought large investments from Latin America—a region that had barely noticed Miami before.

By 1980, when the next wave of Cuban refugees arrived, Miami was a bilingual and bicultural community. Whereas in 1960, 6 percent of the city's population was Hispanic, twenty years later, the figure was 41 percent. Spanish will very soon be the first language of more than half of Miami's residents.

The city was less enthusiastic about the 1980 wave of refugees. This time the refugees had been encouraged to leave Cuba. President Castro's country had suffered agricultural losses and was having difficulty supporting all its citizens. Cuba received massive amounts of financial aid from the Soviet Union, and the Soviets were eager to see an improvement in the country's dire situation. What better way to solve problems than to shoo them out the door? As it turned out, many of those who arrived in the United States had been considered "social problems" in Cuba; some were criminals.

In fact, though, most of the new immigrants were healthy male blue-collar workers, who were eager to work in the United States. Few, however, knew enough English to qualify for jobs.

Florida's Cuban-American community took in these new arrivals, giving them money, clothes, and much-needed advice about living in America. They helped them find jobs, either in Florida or in other parts of the country that had some Cuban Americans.

Still, several years after the second wave of Cuban immigration, not all the refugees have made successful transitions. Many of those who moved north found winters unbearable and came back to south Florida. Many, who'd been told in Cuba to expect a grand welcome in Florida, felt bitterness and despair when life turned out to be very difficult.

In Miami, the new refugees had more trouble in school, at the workplace, and with the law than the earlier arrivals. One reason for the difference is that many of the new arrivals, especially those in their twenties, had never lived in a world of personal freedom and choice. They had always been told what was expected of them and what their choices, if any, were. Now, in a country where motivation and discipline are keys to success, many were failing terribly.

Despite the problems encountered by the 1980 refugees, however, many Cuban Americans are optimistic about their chances for achieving better lives. "This is an exciting community," said one Miami official, "and we're changing every day. The old-timers might not realize it, but this is still the land of opportunity."

The impact of the New Cuban Americans was almost immediate.

Evelyn Cisneros

Prima Ballerina

1958–

W hen Evelyn Cisneros started first grade in the early 1960s in Huntington Beach, California, she was the only Mexican American in her entire school. The other children stared at her and teased her because of her "different" looks. She became painfully shy, afraid even to raise her hand in class. Finally, Evelyn's mother suggested Evelyn take ballet lessons.

Ballet class was a godsend. Her dance teacher, Phyllis Cyr, was struck with both her pupil's natural grace and elegance and her effortless jumps and turns. Soon after Evelyn began her lessons, Ms. Cyr knew she would one day be a wonderful dancer. Evelyn, exhilarated by the challenges of ballet and modern dance, was eager to please her demanding teacher.

Once-a-week lessons soon became daily. To afford more and more classes, Evelyn began teaching beginning classes herself. She also began performing regularly in the evening.

Evelyn's schedule was so demanding that by the time she turned fourteen, she knew she'd have to decide between her commitment to ballet and her life as a normal American school-girl. She loved being with her friends and participating in school activities, but there simply wasn't time for everything. Yet she hated to have to choose between them.

But when she did make a choice, ballet won out. She attended high school from 7:30 A.M. until 2:30 P.M. and then headed for the ballet studio. After dinner at home, she would leave for the Pacific Ballet Theatre in Los Angeles, where she sometimes danced five nights a week.

By her mid-teens, all the hard work was paying off. Evelyn auditioned for the San Francisco Ballet School and received a full scholarship for the summer session. Her first experience with a major ballet company convinced her that she was headed in the right direction.

When Evelyn was sixteen, the San Francisco Ballet School offered to make her an apprentice. She left her school and home in Huntington Beach and in February 1976 moved to San Francisco. Within a year she was invited to become a full-fledged member of the company. At eighteen she had realized her dream—she was a ballerina!

The San Francisco Ballet's artistic director at the time was Michael Smuin. He was drawn to Evelyn's dark beauty and fine technique, and shortly after she joined the company, he created a ballet for her called "A Song for Dead Warriors." This controversial piece about the mistreatment of American Indians showed an eager public the daring and grace of this new ballet star.

Evelyn proved that there was little in San Francisco's repertoire that she couldn't master. In 1981, she danced "The Tempest" for a national television audience. In 1982, President and Mrs. Reagan watched Evelyn dance a selection of ballet and tap numbers at the White House. San Francisco audiences filled the house whenever Evelyn appeared in the double role of Odette/Odile in Swan Lake or as Princess Aurora in "Sleeping Beauty."

Throughout the 1980s, Evelyn Cisneros continued to earn the praise of ballet enthusiasts in her home city and around the world. Critics agree that her exotic beauty and brilliant technique have made her a thoroughly stunning prima ballerina.

Yet Evelyn has not forgotten her schooldays back in Huntington Beach, when she cried because her dark skin and eyes made her too "different" from everyone else. What if my mother hadn't suggested I take ballet lessons, she wonders? Evelyn knows there are many Hispanic children who aren't lucky enough to have strong, resourceful parents—children who will be plagued by shyness and insecurity all their lives. She often speaks to groups of Hispanic schoolchildren about the life of a dancer and the rewards of hard work and determination. She is pleased to think her example will help others turn their own dreams into reality.

Ellen Ochoa

Astronaut

1959–

Ever since 1990 when Dr. Ellen Ochoa was selected to be an astronaut in NASA's Space Shuttle program, Hispanic students and community groups have asked her to speak on her success. Her message is straightforward: "If you stay in school, you have the potential to achieve what you want in the future." Her own example reinforces these words.

Ellen grew up in the San Diego suburb of La Mesa. Her mother, Roseanne, who hadn't had a chance to go to college after high school, enrolled at San Diego State University the year Ellen was born in 1959. Twenty-three years later, after raising four children, Roseanne Ochoa received her bachelor's degree. Ellen took a more direct route, graduating herself from San Diego State before receiving her master's and doctoral degrees in electrical engineering from Stanford.

Before her selection for astronaut training, Ellen was chief of the Intelligent Systems Technology Branch at the NASA/Ames Research Center at Moffet Field Naval Air Station in Mountain View, California. She first applied to NASA in 1985, but it wasn't until 1987 that she was became one of the top one hundred candidates out of more than 2,000 applicants. Finally, in 1990, NASA chose Ellen and twenty-two others to begin training at the Johnson Space Center in Houston, Texas. She was the first Hispanic female ever chosen to become an astronaut.

The training began in October 1990, and in three or four years, Ellen hopes to be assigned to a shuttle flight. Ellen's dream is to build a space station, which she says is "critical . . . to human exploration in space, a transportation mode to new frontiers."

In the meantime, she tries not to lose sight of the frontiers she herself is opening for both women and Hispanics. One of Ellen's role models is the first female astronaut, Sally Ride. Sally, she says, "made it possible for anyone to become an astronaut." And Ellen Ochoa continues to prove that the opportunities for space exploration are indeed limitless.

Training for new astronauts is quite intensive and physically demanding.

Michael Carbajal

Boxer,
Light Flyweight Division

1968–

In a Phoenix neighborhood full of vacant lots and houses that "sort of fall down on their own," Michael Carbajal still works out in the backyard ring built for him by his brother and trainer, Danny. On the front porch of their home sits a barber chair where Danny—also a professional barber—cuts Michael's hair. In fact, life for the Carbajal family doesn't seem to have changed much since the summer of 1990 when Michael became an international boxing star.

Michael Carbajal is small. "Small wonder" and "less is more" are ways that sportswriters describe him. Michael likes to call himself *Manitas de Piedra*, "little hands of stone," which harkens back to his idol, Roberto Duran, who was known as "hands of stone."

Michael weighs 108 pounds, which puts him in the junior, or light, flyweight division. At that weight, he's about half the size of heavyweight boxers. For years, Americans paid little attention to small boxers, heavyweight champions being the ones who made history: Jack Dempsey, Muhammad Ali, Mike Tyson. Most light flyweight champions are Asians or Latin Americans, who are completely unfamiliar to American audiences.

But that's changing now, thanks to Michael Carbajal. His skill, personality, and "hands of stone"—which have considerable punching power—caused NBC to offer him in 1990 a three-year exclusive contract. For the first time, one of the major networks decided to gamble on the little guys. "Once the people see Michael," one promoter observed, "the heavyweights will look terrible, like they were fighting in Jell-O."

All this attention hasn't changed Michael much. He still lives with his parents in their modest home in the Verde Park section of Phoenix. Danny Carbajal lives with his own family in the house next door. As the two become wealthier from Michael's championships and television appearances, they intend to buy up some of the vacant lots in Verde Park and start a gym. Moving out of the neighborhood is not in their plans.

The Carbajal family aren't newcomers to Arizona. They moved north from Mexico during the late nineteenth century—before statehood—and can identify ancestors who fought the Apaches in the long, bloody Indian wars. More recent family history feature's Michael's father, Manuel, who was the state Golden Gloves flyweight champion in the late 1940s. Manuel taught all nine of his children, even the three girls, to box. But only Michael has achieved greatness.

Michael's first boxing award came in the 1981 Southwest Optimist tournament, when he was only fourteen and weighed sixty pounds. Next to it in the Carbajal's trophy case is Michael's Olympic silver medal, won during the 1988 Olympic Games in Seoul, South Korea. Since the Olympics, he's picked up both the North American Boxing Federation's junior flyweight championship and then, in the summer of 1990, the International Boxing Federation world title. In that match, he defeated the former champion, a previously unbeaten boxer from Thailand.

As networks and promoters line up behind Michael Carbajal, the boxer remains modest and soft-spoken. Protected by his close family, he looks forward to more world titles, more contracts, and more publicity for boxing's "little guys." And then he wants to return to "the neighborhood," where life is full of friends and family and mom's home cooking.

Notes

[1]David B. Quinn, ed., *The New American World: A Documentary History of North America to 1612* (New York: Arno Press, 1979).

[2]Cummings et al, eds., *The Discovery of North America* (New York: American Heritage Press, 1972), p. 136.

[3]Gaspar Perez de Villagrá, *Historia de la Nuevo Mexico*, (Alcalá, 1610), in *The Discovery of North America*, eds., Cummings et al, (New York: American Heritage Press, 1972).

[4]Winifred E. Wise, *Fray Junípero Serra and the California Conquest* (New York: Charles Scribner's Sons, 1966), pp. 57–58.

[5]*Ibid.*, p. 59.

[6]*Ibid.*, pp. 60–61.

[7]*Ibid.*, p. 63.

[8]Jacqueline Dorgan Meketa, ed., *Legacy of Honor: The Life of Rafael Chacón, A Nineteenth-Century New Mexican* (Albuquerque: University of New Mexico Press, 1986), p. 1.

[9]*Ibid.*, pp. 165, 168, 169–170.

[10]Loreta Janeta Velázquez, *The Woman in Battle*, as quoted in *Women Adventurers* (New York: Macmillan, 1893).

[11]George Santayana, *Persons and Places: Fragments of Autobiography*, William G. Holzberger and Herman J. Saatkamp, Jr., eds. (Cambridge: The MIT Press, 1986), pp. 129–131.

[12]Mary Fuertes Boynton, ed., *Louis Agassiz Fuertes: His Life Briefly Told and His Correspondence* (New York: Oxford University Press, 1956), p. 307.

[13]Adelina Otero Warren, "The Spell of New Mexico," in *A Documentary History of the Mexican Americans*, Wayne Moquin, ed. (New York: Praeger, 1971), pp. 282–283.

[14]Bernardo Vega, *Memoirs of Bernardo Vega*, Juan Flores, trans., César Andreu Iglesias, ed. (New York: Monthly Review Press, 1984), pp. 3, 6.

[15]*Ibid.*, pp. 21–22.

[16]Mario T. Garcia, *Mexican Americans: Leadership, Ideology and Identity, 1930–1960* (New Haven: Yale University Press, 1989).

[17]Jovita Mireles Gonzales, "With the Coming of Barbed Wire Came Hunger: Folklore of the Texas-Mexican Vaquero," in *Aztlan: An Anthology of Mexican American Literature*, Luis Valdez and Stan Steiner, eds. (New York: Vintage Books, 1972), pp. 80–81.

[18]Luis Alvarez, *Alvarez: Adventures of a Physicist* (New York: Basic Books, 1987), pp. 214.

[19]*Ibid.*, p. 8.

[20]Harold J. Alford, *The Proud Peoples: The Heritage and Culture of Spanish-Speaking Peoples in the United States* (New York: New American Library, 1972), pp. 138–139.

[21]Milton Meltzer, *The Hispanic Americans* (New York: Crowell, 1982), p. 127.

[22]Richard "Poncho" Gonzales, *Man with a Racket* (New York: Barnes, 1959), pp. 38–39.

[23]Reies López Tijerina, in *Aztlan: An Anthology of Mexican American Literature*, Luis Valdez and Stan Steiner, eds. (New York: Vintage Books, 1972).

[24]*Ibid.*

[25]Rodolfo Corky Gonzáles, in *Aztlan: An Anthology of Mexican American Literature*, Luis Valdez and Stan Steiner, eds. (New York: Vintage Books, 1972).

[26]José Angel Gutiérrez, in *Aztlan: An Anthology of Mexican American Literature*, Luis Valdez and Stan Steiner, eds. (New York: Vintage Books, 1972).

[27]Richard Rodriquez, *Hunger of Memory*, (Boston: David R. Godine, 1982), pp. 11–12.

Bibliography

General History and Biography

Anderson, Joan. *Spanish Pioneers of the Southwest*. New York: Lodestar Books E.P. Dutton, 1989. (M)

Conover, Ted. *Coyotes: A Journey Through the Secret World of America's Illegal Aliens*. New York: Vintage, 1987. (U)

Coy, Harold. *Chicano Roots Go Deep*. New York: Dodd, Mead & Co., 1975. (U)

DePaola, Tomie. *The Lady of Guadalupe*. New York: Holiday House, 1980. (E)

Eiseman, Alberta. *Mañana Is Now: The Spanish-Speaking in the U.S.* New York: Atheneum, 1973. (U)

Gerassi, John. *Fidel Castro: A Biography*. Garden City: Doubleday & Co., 1973. (U)

Gillies, John. *Señor Alcalde: A Biography of Henry Cisneros*. Minneapolis: Dillon Press, 1988. (M)

Lawson, Don. *The United States in the Spanish-American War*. New York: Abelard-Schuman, 1976. (U)

Mann, Peggy. *Luis Muñoz Marin: The Man Who Remade Puerto Rico*. New York: Coward, McCann & Geoghegan, Inc., 1976. (U)

Morey Janet and Wendy Dunn. *Famous Mexican Americans*. New York: Cobblehill Books, 1989. (U)

Meltzer, Milton. *The Hispanic American*. New York: Thomas Y. Crowell, 1982. (U)

Newlon, Clarke. *Famous Mexican-Americans*. New York: Dodd, Mead & Co., 1972. (U)

Newlon, Clarke. *Famous Puerto Ricans*. New York: Dodd, Mead & Co., 1975. (U)

Pinchot, Hane. *The Mexicans in America*. Minneapolis: Lerner Publications, 1989. (U)

Tuck, Jay Nelson and Norma C. Vergara. *Heroes of Puerto Rico*. New York: Fleet Press Corporation, 1969. (M)

Williams, Margot and Josephine McSweeney. *Cuba from Columbus to Castro*. New York: Julian Messner, 1982. (M)

Myth, Folk, and Fairy Tales

Belpre, Pura. *The Tiger and the Rabbit and Other Tales*. New York: Frederick Warne & Co., Inc., 1946. (M)

Belpre, Pura. *Perez and Martina*. New York: Frederick Warne & Co., Inc., 1961. (E)

Blackmore, Vivian. *Why Corn Is Golden: Stories about Plants*. Boston: Little Brown, 1984. (E)

Dolch, Edward W. and M. P. Dolch. *Stories from Mexico*. Champaign, IL: Garrard, 1960. (U)

Green, Lila. *Folktales of Spain and Latin America*. Englewood Cliffs: Silver Burdett & Co., 1967. (E)

Hinojosa, Francisco. *The Old Lady Who Ate People: Frightening Stories*. Boston: Little Brown, 1984. (E)

Jagendorf, M.A. and R.S. Boggs. *The King of the Mountain: A Treasury of Latin American Folk Tales*. New York: Vanguard Press, 1960. (M)

Lyons, Grant. *Tales the People Tell in Mexico*. New York: Julian Messner, 1972. (M)

Newman, Shirlee P. *Folk Tales of Latin America*. New York: Bobs-Merrill Company, 1962. (M)

Paredes, Americo. *Folktales of Mexico*. Chicago: The University of Chicago Press, 1970. (U)

Storm, Dan. *Picture Tales from Mexico*. New York: J.B. Lippincott Co., 1941. (M)

E = Easy reading level   M = Middle reading level   U = Upper reading level

Films, Videos, Audiocassettes

The Day It Snowed Tortillas. Joe Hayes. Audiocassette.

Ethnic Holidays. Disney films. Filmstrip and audiocassette, or Video.

Families of the World Series/Mexico. National Geographic. Video or 16 mm film.

Holidays and Celebrations Around the World, Special Times of the Year. National Geographic. Filmstrip and audiocassette.

La Bamba. RCA/Columbia Pictures Home Video. (PG13) Video.

Milagro Beanfield War. MCA Home Video. (R) Video.

Stand and Deliver. An American Playhouse Theatrical Film. Video.

Index

271

Acknowledgments

AP/Wide World Photos: for artist reference 3 front covers; UPI/Bettmann Newsphotos: for artist reference 1 front cover; Historical Pictures Service: ii, v; North Wind Picture Archives: for artist reference 1 front cover, 1, 3, 5; The Bettmann Archive: 8; Culver Pictures, Inc.: 10; North Wind Picture Archives: 12; Historical Pictures Service: 15; North Wind Picture Archives: 16, 18, 20, 22; The Bettmann Archive: 23, 25; Steven Dobson, 28; Courtesy Museum of New Mexico: Gerald Cassidy (Neg #20206) 29; "© Orman Longstreet/SuperStock International, Inc.: 33; Florida State Archives: 35; Historical Pictures Service: 41; New Mexico State Records Center and Archives: A History of New Mexico by Villagra 42; The Bancroft Library: 46; Historical Pictures Service: 47; The Bancroft Library: 51; United States Postal Service: 53; North Wind Picture Archives: 54, 58; California Section, California Library: Photograph Collection — Portola, Gaspar de, Pioneer (Neg. #230) 60; Courtesy of American Jewish Historical Society, UPI/Bettmann Newsphotos: 62; Waltham, Mass.: 65 (right); Courtesy of the Redwood Library, Newport, RI: 65 (left); Rhode Island Historical Society: 67; The Bettmann Archive: 68; Historical Pictures Service: 70; North Wind Picture Archives: 71, 73; Historical Pictures Service: 74; North Wind Picture Archives: 76; ©Gene Ahrens/SuperStock International, Inc.: 77; California Section California Library: Photograph Collection—Early Life: Dance "Fandango" (Neg. #21,066) 80; Courtesy Museum of New Mexico: (Neg #10308) 81; North Wind Picture Archives: 83; Historical Pictures Service: 84; North Wind Picture Archives: 86; Historical Pictures Service: 88; North Wind Picture Archives: 89; Florida State Archives: 92; North Wind Picture Archives: 94; California Section, California Library: Photograph Collection—Early Life: Lassoing; rodeo, etc. (Neg. #3948) 97; Courtesy Museum of New Mexico: (Neg #50815) 98; Historical Pictures Service: 102; Courtesy of Arizona Historical Society/Tucson: (Neg #20957) 103; Courtesy of Colorado Historical Society: 106; Illustration by Oscar Romero: 109, 110; National Archives Trust Fund Board: 113; Historical Pictures Service: 111; California Section California Library: Photograph Collection — Vasquez, Tiburcio, Citizen (Neg.#4412) 114; North Wind Picture Archives: 116; Courtesy of the University of Pennsylvania School of Medicine, University of Pennsylvania Collection of Art, Philadelphia, Pennsylvania:

Murals and the Romero Family

Alejandro Romero 1949–
Oscar Romero 1954–

The paintings of Alejandro Romero pass before the eyes in waves of color and poetry. Music, which he studied in his native Mexico, inspires their intricate compositions. Alejandro's work also draws from history, dance, and film to give a unique interpretation of the immigrant experience.

In one watercolor, which eventually became a poster for the fourth Chicago Latino Film Festival in 1988, the celluloid strips that stream out of a filmmaker's hair mingles with a moving bus and several cars of a Chicago subway as it flows to the edge of the picture. In one corner of the painting, soldiers stand ready for battle next to citizens being held at gunpoint. Unknown to either, their space on the canvas is being overtaken by fire. And, in the painting's foreground, three people dance to a corrido, a Mexican folk ballad.

From his studio in Chicago's Pilsen neighborhood, which was named by Czech immigrants in the early twentieth century, but is now an Hispanic stronghold, Alejandro reflects on his Mexican roots and his native land's culture. He worries that the spirit of Mexican culture is disappearing and he hopes, through his art, to help preserve its most important elements.

When he was six and living in Mexico City, Alejandro was introduced by his grandmother to the great muralist, David Alfaro Siqueiros. Later Alejandro became Siqueiros's assistant, learning about expressionism—which takes art one step past reality—from the great master. Alejandro's brother Oscar also lives in Chicago. They have seven brothers and sisters, all of whom are involved in the art world, working in fashion or advertising or fine arts. Oscar and Alejandro have collaborated on many projects, both in Mexico and in Chicago. In 1978, Oscar joined Alejandro in Chicago and has also become a respected painter. His murals appear in such locations as Loyola University of Chicago, Cook County Correction Facility in Chicago, and at several popular Mexican restaurants. Oscar was commissioned by Childrens Press to design the cover of this book. The mural from which the cover was taken measures more than five feet by eight feet.

The people represented on the cover of the book are representative of those Hispanic Americans who have made important contributions to American culture. Their achievements range from exploration, science, and dance to music, sports, and medicine.

Alejandro Romero   *Oscar Romero*

About the Author

Susan Sinnott began her publishing career as an editor for *Cricket*, a children's magazine. She later worked at the University of Wisconsin Press, where she managed and edited academic journals. Eventually, her own two children pulled her away from the scholarly world and helped her to rediscover the joys of reading, writing, and editing books for young readers. Ms. Sinnott's last book for Childrens Press was *Zebulon Pike*. She now lives in a rattly old house in Portsmouth, New Hampshire, where she is lucky enough to be able to sit at her desk and look out at the lovely harbor.